Yoruba
16 Oracle Geomancy

Sixto J. Novaton
(BabaSixto IfaOdara)

blue ocean press
tokyo - florida

Published by:
blue ocean press, an imprint of Aoishima Research Institute (ARI)

Main Office (US): P.O. Box 510818, Punta Gorda 33951
Rep. Office: #807-36 Lions Plaza Ebisu , 3-25-3 Higashi, Shibuya-ku,
Tokyo, Japan 150-0011

Email: mail@aoishima-research.org

URL: http://www.blueoceanpublications.com
       http://www.aoishima-research.org

ISBN: 978-4-902837-16-2

Table of Contents

Illustrations

1
0
1
1

0
1
0
1

0
1
0
0

1
0
1
1

0
1
0
1

0
1
0
0

How to read the coconut toss:
Obtaining an oracle for divination

This simple system is a summarized extract of accumulated knowledge from when I first began to toss obi (coconuts) at 16. Granted, it has been expanded with insights from the cowrie (dilogun) and Ifá systems of divination. It has been written for those who after having dedicated much time to spiritual enlightenment, now have a need to verify their communication through a simple 'yes' or 'no' questioning system, plus a more elaborate simple binary extension. Plainly, there are those who do not have an affinity with any divination system. So, I have put together this system of 16 basic signs that will support the communication necessary for any individual to obtain answers. The rest is up to the individual's merited grace and intuition. This system will also expand an individual's medium development through devotion and practice.

To be utilized are four circular coconut shells, 4 coins, or 4 cowrie shells (see figure 010). The objects need to be of the same type, shape, and one side can be identified as facing upward (1), and the bottom side (0). The written format is indicative of the toss being read from bottom to top, and right to left. For the sake of maintaining this system simple i.e. (not limiting to any specific set of divinities) all divinities, which an individual has forged a relationship through their merits will speak to them through this system. All that is needed is an invocation prayer, which they have an affinity with in order to call upon them through an established relationship.

Helpful Advice: Never take interpretations ultra-literally. There are moments when you will be on point; and other moments when you need to concentrate and allow for situations to develop for you to understand the message. Attempt to apply from each sign what is relevant to what you are living at that moment. Yet, always remember that you are where you are based on causes and effects from your past; i.e. decisions and choices you have made are what have put you in the predicaments that you are experiencing today. This system forms a base towards the learning of the more complex Yoruba Lucumi systems of divination, especially for those wishing to continue into priesthood in Yoruba-Lucumi-Santeria spiritual-intellectual tradition. It will not replace the proficiency of divination performed by a fully qualified Yoruba Orisha, or Ifa priest. At times when one is in need of specialized ritual work for solving difficult situations in life, please see a qualified individual.

Note: Those wishing to read on a mat, should use consecrated coins or shells, preferably shells. For tossing on the floor, use the coconut shells

Consecration of religious objects for divination

Find a religious pagan, or Santeria/Ifa priest practitioner, who can consecrate your divination objects 4 coins, 4 coconut shells, or 4 cowrie shells.

Find a religious pagan, or Santeria/Ifa priest practitioner, which can help you consecrate or formulate a spiritual altar, or shrine space for spiritual practice.

Place the consecrated objects on your shrine, and proceed to spiritual devotion through weekly prayer and meditation ritual. An individual needs to put in the time in attaining spiritual grace, enlightenment, and merit the divine forces attention. This is no overnight task. It can take months and years of devotion in order to merit the correct communication. Always look to receive mentorship from an experienced priest-ess. It is imperative that you do, so as to not open a can of worms, and then not know how to resolve situations.

The time will come for you to experiment. I am of the belief in obtaining experience, and getting to know your spiritual connection to divinities and forces on your own, but through much guidance and discipline. There is no one better than yourself who knows of your life struggles, which leads to an understanding of whom your spirit guides are. Yet, without mentorship many more mistakes can be made leading to slower development, so never stop trying to find the right person to connect with. When working to achieve meeting the right mentor, pray and meditate to your ancestors and spirit guides to lead you to the correct person.

Way of Using the System

Have a special mat that will be used exclusively for tossing your objects onto. Place a glass of water next to it. Then proceed to reciting your invocation prayer as accustomed and according to the belief system in which you are obtaining training or being mentored. Included here is a Yoruba mojuba, as well as a spiritual prayer, which I used many years ago when I used to cast the I-Ching coins. Then proceed to tossing the objects:

Ways of Tossing

First Way

Ask a question then toss the objects to obtain a simple "Yes" or "NO" by just reading the sign as 1 of 5 answers; the answers being Alafia, Eyeife, Itawa, Okana Sodde, or Okana Yekun. Only take the advice from above relative to what has been written for these names. Do not interpret it as an oracle. Continue, asking simple yes or no, or give thanks and stop.

Second Way

This way requires you to read the signs named "Oracles."

You toss the coins asking a question about what you would like to know, or if you do not ask any question it is what advice you would need to have at this time.
Proceed by tossing the first Oracle and writing it down. Then, toss the second oracle and write it down. Finally, toss the third oracle and writing it down.

13

When tossing the coins always remember to read the signs by looking at the objects from closest to you to furthest to you. Reading a 1 or 0, from bottom to top.

How to Interpret

The first oracle is the name of what you are living at the moment. The second and third sign is the direction in which to take the first sign. In essence, the conversation relative to the situations involving the first sign.

After reading the oracles you can then ask simple "Yes" and "No" questions and answers to clarify your position relative to the oracles.

Once obtaining an oracle some will ask, "what do I do to better or support positive changes in my life, according to what I just read?"

Advice: talk to a religious elder for recommendations or clarifications. This is a system for aspiring priest to obtain wisdom, practice and guidance. This system along with the guidance of an elder will support positive communication with an elder, which can lead to positive spiritual growth and development.

Always close at the end, with giving thanks, for the communication. Also, if you get stuck, do not hesitate to obtain wisdom from a more experienced elder, mentor, or guide; Many blessings to all, BabaSixto (IfaOdara) Aboru, Aboye, Aboshe-she.

Invocation Prayer

Hymn 15 (from the book on the Dead Sea Scrolls)

I thank Thee, O Lord, and nothing exists except by Thy will; none can consider [Thy deep secrets] or contemplate Thy [mysteries]. What then is man that is earth, that shaped [from clay] and return to the dust, that Thou shouldst gave him to understand such marvels and make knows to him the counsel of [Thy truth]? Clay and dust that I am, what can I devise unless Thou wish it, and what contrive unless Thou desire it? What strength shall I have unless Thou keep me upright, and how shall I understand unless by (the spirits) which Thou hast shaped for me? What can I say unless Thou open my mouth and how can I answer unless Thou enlighten me? Behold, Thou art Prince of gods and King of majesties, Lord of all spirits, Ruler of all creatures; nothing is done without Thee, and nothing is known without Thy will. Beside Thee there is nothing, and nothing can compare with Thee is strength; in the presence of Thy glory there is nothing, and Thy might is without price. Who among Thy great and marvelous creature can stand in the presence of Thy glory? How then can, he who returns to his dust? For Thy glory's sake alone hast Thou made all these things.

Lucumi Mojuba Prayer

Ashe Omi tutu, ona tutu, tutu ile ni Olodumare, Tutu talabi
Iba Baba, Iba Yeye, Iba Sherda, Iba Korda, Iba Orishabi.
Iba Irunmole Oju kotun, Iba igbamole Oju kosi
Iba Okanle ni-irinwo Irunmole
Iba Irawo, Iba Oshupa
Iba Atiyo ojo, Iba Atiwo orun
Iba Ile Oguere a-foko yeri

Iba Adechina, Iba Tanda, Iba Kaide, Iba Ifaomi.

Iba Yen ba yen tonu Bogbo Egun Arae, Abata, Shebo,
Orimi, Timbelaiye, timbelese Olodumare

Iba Yen tonu... (insert names of ancestors, relatives, and
deceased religious elders, as per your house lineage).

Iba Yen tonu, and blessings from spiritual guides and
ancestors of my religious elders... (insert names of your
religious elders).

Iba yen ba yen tonu Bogbo Iya-losha, Baba-losha, toku,
Awo toku, apetebi, iworo toku timbelaiye timbelese
Olodumare Ariku Baba-wa

Iba-She Olodumare; Ibashe Olofin; ibashe Olorun; Ibashe
Elerda

Iba-She Emi Oluo Siwayu, Ojubona kan
Iba-She Iyalosha tobi, baba losha tobi
Iba-she Bogbo Iworo, Awofaka, Apetebi Kowa-nile....
Ariku Baba-wa

Mojuba Eshu Baralayiki eduerona komani komani kondo a la ilu
Mojuba Ogun loko mariwo yeye
Mojuba Odede Lokuo, karele oniyo Oshosi
Mojuba Osuduru madubule duru ganga-laboshe Osun
Mojuba Inle Agbata chelewe-ni, Alaga-nao Koikoto
Mojuba OrishaOko Iku Afefe
Mojuba Osain, ObaluAye Asowano
Mojuba Dada Banyani, Ibeji bejilawo Ideu
Mojuba Agaju Shola kiniba Oroinya
Mojuba Shango Kabiosile
Mojuba Obatala Obataisa Obatayano
Mojuba Yewa, Oba ya-osi
Mojuaba Yanza akata jeri jey mesa
Mojuba Yemaja Obinilateo
Mojuba Iyare mi agoyo Olokum
Mojuba Oshun Yeye Kari Yalorde
Mojuba Orunmila Ake meji awa lori, Ifa Lowo, Ifa Loma Ariku Baba-Iwa

Emi Omo re ... (insert your name here).... kio wa ma she o, fu mi ashe
Kosi Iku, Kosi Arun, Kosi Ofo, Kosi Ejo... Ariku Baba-wa
Fun mi Ire Ariku, Ire Aye, Ire Dewantolokum, Ire Ashegun Ota.... Ariku Baba iwa.

Examples of How to Interpret Signs

Example 1 (Busines Question):
"Is xxxx (name) the correct contractor for restoration of properties back in my home country?"

First toss:	0	Oyekun – Eyioko – Cowrie (2)
	0	
	0	
	0	
2nd toss	1	Eyeife – Iroso – Cowrie (4)
	1	
	0	
	0	
3rd toss	0	Okana Sodde - Ika - Cowrie (14)
	1	
	0	
	0	

Note: Only pick out the info from the advices that are pertinent to the question or reason for doing the reading.

First cast Oyeku - so you look in the booklet and read Oyekun **"As an Oracle"**

"As an oracle it signifies the land of the dead mother earth. Where everything dies, decomposes, becomes nourishment for life to regenerate all over again. It is an oracle of materialism, abundance, being greedy, and change. It is to take care of yourself so that blessing is not short lived or fall apart in front of you. It is an oracle of being indebted to the divinities. Promises must be kept; there are unfinished, or undone spiritual labors/tasks that need to be completed before other changes can transpire. It is an oracle of knowing how to be obedient, listen, and take advice; or suffer the consequences of failure. **It means take your time and do the things right.** Oyekun is to never think you know more then the Forces. It is one of adhering to the rules and hierarchy of divinities, spiritual, and physical (natural) worlds. Know your position, your role, and perform your duties as expected. It is an oracle of supporting, and the expansion of family. **Know that your actions can benefit,** as well as, hurt others, especially family."

Then, you toss two more times: and you read for those other two:

1   Eyeife - Iroso – Cowrie (4)
1
0
0

Iroso means the unknown, mysterious, occult, and surprises. It is to avoid entrapments, or made part of grander scheme. Iroso has a saying, "No one knows the mysteries which lie beneath the debts of the seas": as in a blessing, which can come out of nowhere; as well as, trouble when taken in negative context. **It is an oracle of discovery as much as it is of danger of business takeovers, being jacked, risky business; as it is of risk which lands a score or jackpot.** It marks life coming to an end regarding a terminal illness. The person needs to work diligently with the divinities, Orisha, and ancestors to avoid accidents, fires, and diseases anything that can lead to shortening their stay here. **Advice: avoid crooked people; where people try to make a living out of illegal means –** "If you can't do the time - don't do the crime."

0	Okana Sodde - Ika - Cowrie (14)
1	
0	
0	

Ika means to know how to get around things, situations; or finding your way. It is the need to obtain stability. If the individual has been thrown out, expelled, or lost their stability. They need to work diligently performing all the necessary rituals or spiritual work to get to where they need to be. It is imperative that they find a new job, home, mate, or start over a family. **Ika is an oracle of a time of battle and the work that needs to be done to win. Ika is an oracle of going on the road towards finding ones profession,** and the city or town where one is going to be successful. Where you are at the time might not be the correct place. This is why you are struggling so much. Not to get into a witchcraft war or power struggle with anyone.

You read the three and relate them to the question you asked. Then, you get rid of any doubts in your interpretations by asking questions to obtain a direct "Yes" or "No" response. This is where you take the advice of the simple toss.

Interpretation:
Oyekun - It is good that you are doing things to help the land, yourself, and family.

21

Iroso - If the person is crooked and not trustworthy, then you can lose. If the person is good, then all things will be done well. Also, while you are not there, you will be taking a risk with whomever anyway.

Ika - If the person you are asking about has no stability, has been fired or let go from their job; they need money. So, if the job is not being done, it is because they are using some of your money for their expenses. If they have money, they do not need your money, and the money you send will be allocated to the project.

Based on this you would ask - "Is the contractor a good contractor?

If yes, then does he need more money to do a good job?

If yes, once I give him more money will all renovations go according to plan?

If No, he's not a good contractor.

If No, once I give him more money the renovations won't get done?

Then, according to the signs, you have to find another contractor.

Example 2 (Relationship Question):
Question: "Does xxxx (name) make a good romantic partner for me?"

First toss	0	Eyeife - Ofun - Cowrie (10)
	1	
	0	
	1	

2nd toss	1	Eyeife - Iroso – Cowrie (4)
	1	
	0	
	0	

3rd toss	0	Eyeife - Ofun - Cowrie (10)
	1	
	0	
	1	

Toss 1: Main topic

	0	Eyeife - Ofun - Cowrie (10)
	1	
	0	
	1	

Ofun is an oracle of self defense; where defending yourself is permitted. It is an oracle of great wisdom, growth, and grandeur. Yet, not to allow the grandeur to get one's head, so as not to suffer failures. It is an oracle of perfection, and balance. Again like all greatness without humility, without understanding limitations, demise follows. It is the oracle of understanding death, and that all endings are a new beginning. What death represents, the land of the dead, working with the dead, elevation of the dead, ancestor worship. This oracle personifies living in harmony with society, nature, and your surroundings - Tao. It is where God's Messengers/ Holy Scriptures/ Word enters the world to teach mankind how to better live. Signifies losing one's life by overstepping one's position, disobedience, risk, or imposing will for selfish gain. What comes to mind with this oracle is "You're only as strong as the next person, who is equal to you or stronger."

Toss 2: Conversation relating to Main topic
1   Eyeife - Iroso – Cowrie (4)
1
0
0

Iroso means the unknown, mysterious, occult, and surprises. It is to avoid entrapments, or made part of grander scheme. Iroso has a saying, "No one knows the mysteries which lie beneath the depths of the seas." As in a blessing which can come out of nowhere, as well as, trouble when taken in negative context. It is an oracle of discovery as much as it is of danger of business takeovers, being jacked, risky business, as it is of risk which lands a score, or jackpot. It marks life coming to an end regarding a terminal illness. The person needs to work diligently with the divinities, Orisha, and ancestors to avoid accidents, fires, and diseases; anything that can lead to shortening their stay here. Advice: avoid crooked people; where people try to make a living out of illegal means - "If you can't do the time - don't do the crime."

Toss 3: Closing Argument or Outcome

      0   Eyeife - Ofun - Cowrie (10)
      1
      0
      1

Ofun is an oracle of self defense, where defending yourself is permitted. It is an oracle of great wisdom, growth, and grandeur. Yet, not to allow the grandeur to get one's head, so as not to suffer failures. It's an oracle of perfection, and balance. Again like all greatness without humility, without understanding limitations, demise follows. It is the oracle of understanding death, and that all endings are a new beginning. What death represents, the land of the dead, working with the dead, elevation of the dead, ancestor worship. This oracle personifies living in harmony with society, nature, and your surroundings - Tao. It is where God's Messengers/ Holy Scriptures/ Word enters the world to teach mankind how to better live. Signifies losing one's life by overstepping one's position, disobedience, risk, or imposing will for selfish gain. What comes to mind with this oracle is "You're only as strong as the next person, who is equal to you or stronger."

To summarze:

Ofun - Not to allow the relationship to go to one's head. To take a balanced approach to relationship. Harmonizing as getting to know how each other lives within society, and surroundings. Are you both ready to live together to see if you can harmonize, or take things slow?

Iroso - Still a realm of the unknown, yet open up so that there no mysteries in the relationship. Whatever is hidden must come out. If there are still ties to an ex-, all ties must be severed. Any court cases, or legal issues involved in, to always be clear. No surprises later as in "you never told me before." Discovery - you still need to learn more about each other. This is a fragile oracle because anything wrong that one does or says to the other can cause the romance to die. It is always risky when one attempts to become romantically involved with another.

Ofun - Defend your position with reasons as to the "whys?" relative to situations in your life (of course when in dialogue). In Ofun, each others' limitations are to be known. One is to not impose will on the other. Both have to put in the time and effort to make the relationship a good and lasting one.

After summarizing all other questions are answered through the toss where yes is yes, and no is no. Not to look at the tosses any further as an oracle, so as not to confuse the original advice. "Yes's" are (Alafia, Eyeife, Itawa Meji), and "No's" are (Okana sodde, and Oyekun).

The 16 Oracles of
Yoruba Lucumi Geomancy

Alafia
Ogbe - Unle - Cowrie (8)

1
1
1
1

As, a simple toss (all heads):

Yes - thank you, health, and happiness; perfect answer when having placed an offering or libation to a divinity and wishing to verify that it has been well received. When having asked a question, it is also interpreted as "Yes" thank you for asking. Alafia, also represents wisdom, and great spirituality; but most of all, good health and things being on path.

Read as an Oracle - (8)
1
1
1
1

Alafia can be interpreted as Ogbe/Unle - the head, which carries the body. So you think, so you are; where your mind takes you, so there will you be. From a positive point of you, it is to be proud of how far you've come. It is to be on track with achieving goals, and to see things through. On a negative thought, once you've reached the top, the worst that can happen is one falling, or suffering losses. Speaks of separations, and adaption to change after having made a decision that took you in the wrong direction. It advises not to lose your head, i.e. give in to negative ego, or impulses. It recommends patience and protective actions. If your time is up where you are, then it is time to move on; life is a long road, which never ends. Speaking in Ogbe are all situations dealing with the mind, thoughts, wisdom, confrontations, and not overstepping boundaries. Separations lead to new beginnings. Beware of actions that can turn into justice situation, or lead to incarceration. But most of all, to be organized or bringing order to your life. This is an oracle of being saved by taking a leap of faith and entering a spiritual practice. Ogbe is also, road, path, and to be elevated to a new position.

Itawa

1	1	1	0
1	1	0	1
1	0	1	1
0	1	1	1
(3)	(13)	(16)	(9)

Simple toss (3 heads and 1 tail) means:

Almost - "Yes" or "Maybe" a subsequent toss is merited in order to obtain an Alafia, Eyeife, Okana Sodde, Okana Yekun, or another Itawa. Itawa has a saying, "Why ask what you already know the answer to." Itawa also says, "It's perfect to know that there's nothing perfect; that's why it's perfect." Itawa regarding ritual is obtained when a divinity is accepting the work being done, although it could have been done with more accuracy, detail, or better organization or substances. It is a sign of work to be continued as in it's not over yet. Itawa indicates follow up work at a later date to reassure that things are going in the correct path. There might be other divinities that would like to contribute to the success of the work being done. This is a sign that requires followup and continued work.

As the various Oracles:

Ogunda - Cowrie (3)

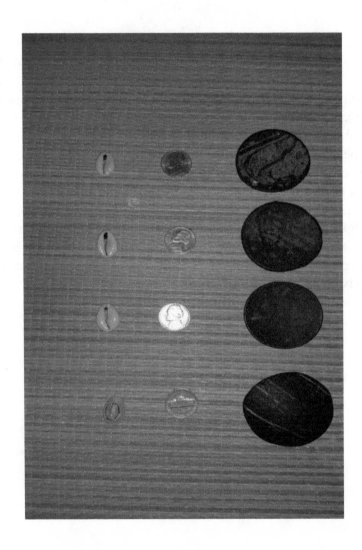

1
1
1
0

This is an oracle of being dedicated to a profession, as well as safeguarding your position, title, work, or livelihood. It is to avoid putting your freedom at risk, i.e. justice situation. Avoid putting your life at risk through physical altercations, or quarreling. It is an oracle of fights, and robbery, or use of force. Never take advantage of the weak, mistreat others; or you'll suffer being mistreated. Someone needs protection in winning a battle, or court case. Speaks of domestic violence, and trying to obtain things by force. One needs to be tenderer regarding different relationships; lighten up, and become sweeter. Of course, unless you're in a battle, in which case, the oracle is perfect because it is one for fighting. But, most of all, one needs to find peace. The greatest asset of Ogunda is to become educated – because ignorance will lead to hardship.

Irete - Cowrie (13)

1
1
0
1

Irete is an oracle of being sought after looked for or found. Beware of investigations, or someone snooping. It also represents an escape, climbing out of hole, getting out of a rut. When desperate or in despair there is someone or a situation will arise where one will obtain the needed support – towards overcoming the difficulty. It is an oracle of upward mobility as in stepping up a ladder. It is one of physical challenges, and being aware of not falling and fracturing one's limbs. When it comes to women, this is a sign that relates to difficult pregnancies. Beware of love triangles and promiscuity, which can lead to STD's. Learning how to attend to spirit guides and ancestors is important because it is a sign that marks communications with them. Learn to be obedient and listen to ancestral advises. There will be a reunion or gathering soon. The person is need of much love, romanticism, or seeking the correct love of their life.

Otura - Cowrie (16)

1
0
1
1

Otura speaks of living in an inhospitable place. It is to be surrounded, or living among con artists and thieves. Also, to avoid being conned or tricked; someone is to be outwitted. Never be the first to know, or know the most; and the last to take advantage of opportunities. To not be given recognition, to falling asleep – not being sharp. Don't lax or take your time about things. Resolve things quickly and swiftly. When being too slow to move, react, or get things done will lead to losses. Closure needs to be put to all things in order for them not to bite you in the end. Oracle of knowing how to live within your means; respect and worship the forces of God. Depending on how well an individual works with the divine forces, so will their grace bring them blessings. Speaks of dark forces robbing the person's luck, happiness, and economic well-being.

Osa - Cowrie (9)

0
1
1
1

Osa is an oracle which signifies things being up in the air. Things that are up for grabs, unsure, or insecure. Religious work needs to be done in order to solidify marriage, job, health, and family. Not all things can be manipulated or resolved through witchcraft or working spells. We can be our own worst enemy by being willful, selfish, and wanting things our way, in spite of the greater good of things. Obstacles occur due to not giving what is necessary to the divinities. All divinities and forces merit their fare share of attention. Spirit guides and ancestors need to be given light, especially those, who have died tragic or recent. Recently deceased, as well as, living individuals need to come out of the darkness and into the light given understanding of their status. Individuals need to open their eyes and be made aware of the truth behind situations. Not to be cheap. There are investments and business in time that will get better staying consistent, and not giving up. Osa also is light; to enlighten; to give or obtain enlightenment. Trying to get over on people unjustly is Osa's greatest failure. If money is not managed properly, you are sure to struggle.

Eyeife
1100(4) - 1010(5) - 1001(7) - 0101(10) - 0110(15) - 0011(11)

1	1	1	0	0	0
1	0	0	1	1	0
0	1	0	0	1	1
0	0	1	1	0	1
(4)	(5)	(7)	(10)	(15)	(11)

Simple Toss (2 heads 2 tails) Eyeife means:

"Yes" affirmative, all will be resolved. The work being done is correct, and exact. Also, a good outcome to situations sought. Differs from the Alafia's "Yes," which in comparison demands correct action to not lose blessings. Differs from Itawa's "Yes," where it is work in progress and followup with more work. Eyeife shows things coming to pass. It is the coming to completion of efforts taken in resolve. Itawa's come before Eyeife as indicators of resolve. Alafia's come after Eyeife, in appreciation of having faith in the divinities. Eyeife is to be on track with meeting one's objective.

As the various Oracles:

Eyeife - Iroso – Cowrie (4)

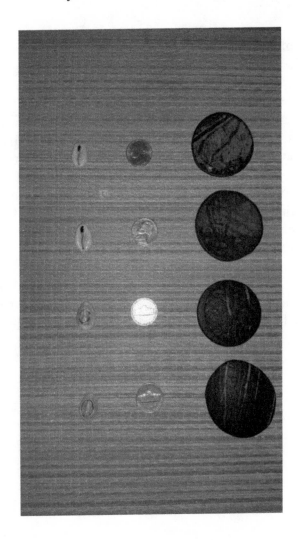

1
1
0
0

Iroso means the unknown, mysterious, hidden, secrecy, and surprises. It is to avoid entrapments; or made part of grander scheme. Iroso has a saying, "No one knows the mysteries which lie beneath the depths of the seas." As in a blessing that can come out of nowhere; as well as, trouble when taken in negative context. It is an oracle of discovery as much as it is of danger of business takeovers; being jacked; risky business; as it is of risk taken for landing a score, or hitting a jackpot. It marks life coming to an end regarding a terminal illness – or having short life. The person needs to work diligently with the divinities, Orisha, and ancestors to avoid accidents, fires, and diseases anything that can lead to sudden fall, illness, or death. Advice: avoid crooked people; where people try to make a living out of illegal means – "If you can't do the time – don't do the crime." If you like a dangerous life - then assume responsibilitie for actions, and accept the consequences of decisions made.

Oshe - Eyeife - Cowrie (5)

1
0
1
0

This is an oracle of fights over money, and in some cases over livelihood (bringing food to your table). Oracle of being cheated. It is the oracle where money is cursed. It is a curse because it is only satisfied as an entity with the blood, sweat, and tears of human souls. The rich folks curse is not to lose it; the poor folks curse is in not having it. Oshe is an oracle that also marks the decomposition of things (falling apart) due to uncleanliness, disease, or filthiness - hence it is an oracle of sanitizing, washing, and expunging. Speaks of blood disorders. Dysfunctional or disorganized family and affairs. The protection of family, affairs, issues, and economic well being. The gain of good graces (spirituality), or loss of your spirituality or gift. Protect that which you've worked so hard to maintain. Love God and his divinities so you attend them, so will they support you in getting out of situations and resolving. Oshe is an oracle of needing to be saved by taking the leap of faith and entering priesthood/brotherhood.

Odi - Eyeife - Cowrie (7)

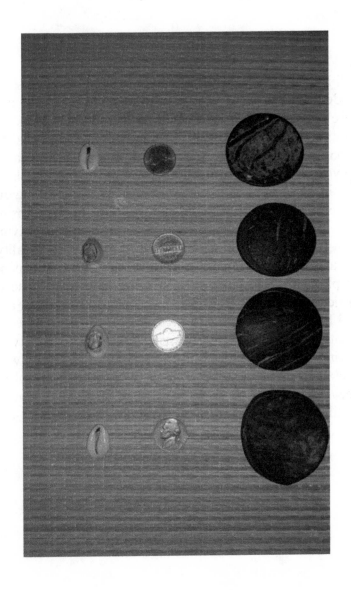

1
0
0
1

Odi is an oracle of great luck, and of having a strong spirit guide, and ancestor link that when used properly and developed - great things happen in the person's life. Yet, they can be a bit obnoxious overbearing, or surrounded by obnoxious overbearing people and things. The greatest downfall in the person's life according to this oracle is gossip, being nosy, and false witnessing. Also, speaking out of content, or giving out information to the wrong individuals at the wrong time. It is an oracle of having some sort of habit or addiction, i.e., addictive personality. Speaks of the creation of the marketplace; not to over spend on pleasures. Substance abuse and alcoholism will lead to justice situations, losses, imprisonment, bad behaviors, and bad character. Keeping a marriage is difficult due to emotional imbalances, or jealousy issues. Speaks of having having been traumatized as a youth. Getting alone with one's own family can be difficult. Where family members become enemies of each other. The ancestors demand family unity. Avoid indecisiveness, selfishness, and promiscuity.

Ofun - Eyeife - Cowrie (10)

0
1
0
1

Ofun is an oracle of self defense, where defending yourself is permitted. It is an oracle of great wisdom, growth, and grandeur. Yet, not to allow the grandeur to get one's head, so as not to suffer failures and setbacks. It is an oracle of perfection, and balance. Again greatness without humility, or knowing limitations will lead to demise and destruction. It is the oracle of understanding death, and that all endings are a new beginning. What death represents, the land of the dead, working with the dead, elevation of the dead, ancestor worship. This oracle personifies living in harmony with society, nature, and your surroundings - Tao. It is where God's messengers/holy scriptures/word enters the world to teach mankind how to better live. Signifies losing one's life by overstepping one's position, disobedience, risk, or imposing will for selfish gain. What comes to mind with this oracle is "You're only as strong as the next person, who is equal to you or stronger."

Iwori - Eyeife - Cowrie (15)

0
1
1
0

Iwori means to be good, yet what is the opposite of good, to
be evil. To never think you know more than God, his
divinities, and the land of the dead. It is the oracle of
scientific discovery, technology, psychology, and all
around wisdom. Yet, of maintaining a level head and not
allowing things to go to your head, or you'll go crazy,
suffer mental breakdown, or end up alone. Where
privileged individuals can lose everything being over
confident, and making willful mistakes; they need to listen
to others too – in respect to elder's advice. The greatest
challenge is to learn how to obtain things by the grace of
God, and divinities. This demands great patience and
allowing the divinities to bring things to you. Iwori's battle
for a position; battle to leave their mark on life and obtain
recognition. Where families destroy one another or support
one another, and are a force to be reckoned with.

Ojuani - Eyeife - Cowrie (11)

0
0
1
1

Ojuani means from riches to rags, and from rags to riches. It is an oracle of doubting, yet overzealous ambition; which when not stopped becomes destructive. Beware of imposing will upon others. Learn to live with others in peace; strive for an education, obtaining a career, profession, or title. To be responsible and not careless throwing things to chance. Oracle of becoming easily bored with mates, so beware of promiscuity and STD's. People lose due to jealousy, and envy even within family. Speaks of dark forces getting in the way of progress, external or internal. Oracle marks needing to be exorcised of dark forces when prevalent – as in being haunted, or sucked dry by negative energies. This is sign is where your mate's family can be your worst enemy or your greatest asset.

Okana Sodde

0	0	0	1
0	0	1	0
0	1	0	0
1	0	0	0
(01)	(12)	(14)	(06)

Simple toss (3 tails 1 head) means:

A straight "No," - don't, not this, something else and stop - check on something else desired at the time, or something is not correct at the time according to what you are asking. Many don't like to receive a "No" when asking or performing ritual work, yet how can divinities tell you what to change or switch with a "Yes"? So, the "No" is a good indicator of the divinities communicating with you and specifying how they want things done. It is not always that "No" means not to do something, it can also mean stop change the order of things, or find the best path. "No" can also mean it is not the proper time for obtaining desires; energies in your surroundings are not positively aligned or conducive to favoring your actions at this moment. Also, there may be other rituals or much more work needed to be done for positive outcome. With tossing an Itawa before followed by an Okana, it's obvious that it means "Maybe + No" ask for something else, in another way, or something is missing; there's a need to add more things - things are unsure.

Okana as Oracles:

Okana - Okana Sodde - Cowrie (1)

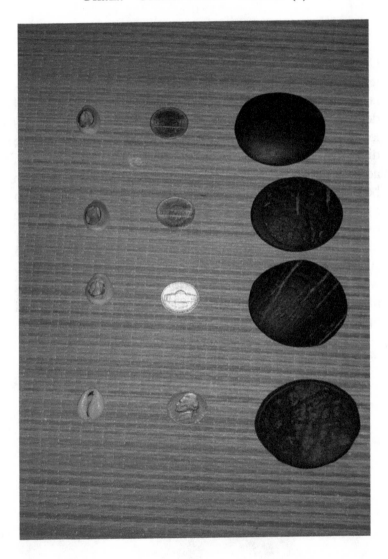

0
0
0
1

Okana is to be roped, bound, or tied. Speaks of letting go of things that keep and individual bounded. Also means needing to bind or secure something so as not to lose it. All depends on situation and where the communication is leading to. Never do things without the consent of the divinities. Okana specifically speaks of all types of addictions; sexual, substance, chemical, shopping – that can be destructive. Oracle of habits: acquire good habits; let go of bad ones. Okana is a drought; of course, if you overconsume you will be left without. Speaks of only remembering God and divinities in times of necessity, or to suit their purpose. Then, when not obtaining what they want, not believing that spirituality exists or works. Speaks of being dumb or stubborn – needing understanding and open-mindedness. Okana is an oracle of atmospheric changes, or going out in bad weather. Also, wrong place wrong time; right place right time.

0
0
1
0

Otrupon is to be offended, to offend, or someone is on the offense. Implying the need to protect yourself. It is also to get rid of the traumatic effects of being embarrassed or offended. Speaks of wanting out of a relationship, situation, job; and unable to find the way out. There is someone that wants to takeover, or win everything at all cost. They would do whatever it takes to get someone out of their way, and obtain their means. Not to give into selfishness, ego, or pride; also to never be prejudiced, misjudge, nor persecute anyone unjustly. Speaks of family betraying one another. Where mates in battle want to destroy one another. After the storm comes peace. With Otrupon one has to be very intelligent not to lose, because there is a tendency of being overconfident.

Ika - Okana Sodde - Cowrie (14)

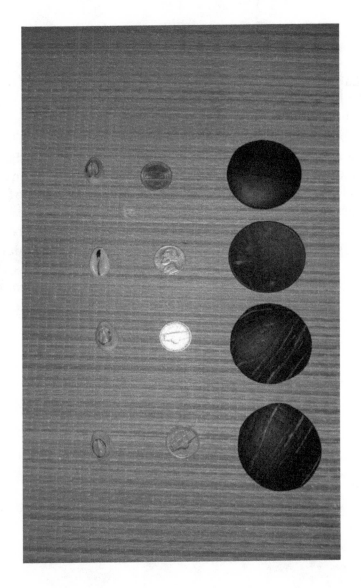

0
1
0
0

Ika means to know how to get around situations, things, or finding your way. It is the need to obtain stability. If the individual has been thrown out, expelled, or lost their stability, they need to work diligently performing all the necessary rituals, or spiritual work to get to where they need to be. It is imperative that they find a new job, home, mate, or start over with a new family. Ika is an oracle of a time of battle, and the work that needs to be done to win. Ika is an oracle of going on the road towards finding one's profession, city/town, where one is going to be successful. At the time, you might not be in the correct place. This is why one is struggling so much. Not to get into a witchcraft war, or power struggle with others; allow elders or more experienced people to help and support you.

Obara - Okana Sodde - Cowrie (6)

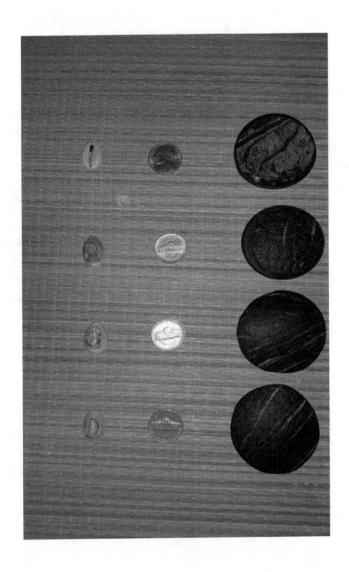

1
0
0
0

Obara says, "There can't be change without revolution, chaos, or torment." An oracle of wisdom, intelligence, and learning how to better live or coexist with your environment. Obara is an oracle where being proud leads to starvation, being left alone, or put to the side. Oracle of success or failure, where the tongue, verb, or speaking can save you or do you in. The tongue can be used for evil, as it can be used for good. Good when it is used to praise, and pray for good things. Evil went it is used to offend and false witness. So, mind your tongue. Speaks of knowing how not to fall after having gained and moved up in life. Speaks of good business relations when fair. Speaks of difficulties in maintaining relationships (personal, social) due to being difficult to satisfy. Not to be a liar; there's no honor in lying. This is an oracle of conquering.

Oyekun
Okana Yekun - Eyioko - Cowrie (2)

0
0
0
0

Simple reply (4 tails) means:

"No" with consequences; when tossing to an Orisha, and the first toss yields this sign. The Orisha is stating that there is spirit guide or ancestor requiring attention prior to the Orisha being able to accept the ritual that you are doing at the moment with them. So, stop check to see what the land of the dead is requiring, then return to the Orisha. If not communicating with an Orisha, and the answer is "No" - then it is negative with consequences. There are times when a divinity will give you all four down as a form of getting your attention in order for you to focus on other pressing matters. In this case continue asking on the various topics prevalent to you, until you hit upon the topic. Then, divert your attention back to your original questioning. Please, note that bargaining with a divinity cannot exist. Many people do try, not understanding that logic dictates "Yes" equal positive, "No" is negative. Because, a divinity cannot give you what you desire does not mean that the divinities do not work. It is just that your request is not within reason at the moment. Who is to say what conditions need to be met in the physical world for your situation to be resolved? Always try to think as to why the answer would be "No"; imagine being in the position of a divinity and ask yourself the question – you will be surprised how many times you would already know the answer before asking. When getting stuck, look to advice from an elder.

As an Oracle:
Oyekun – Eyioko (2)

0
0
0
0

As an oracle it signifies the land of the dead, mother earth. Where everything dies, decomposes, becomes nourishment for life to regenerate all over again. It is an oracle of materialism, abundance, being greedy, and change. It is to take care of yourself choices and decisions made, so that blessing do not fall short, or lost. It is an oracle of being indebted to the divinities. Promises must be kept; there are unfinished, or undone spiritual labors/tasks that need to be completed before other changes can transpire. It is an oracle of knowing how to be obedient, listen, and take advice, or suffer the consequences of failure. It means take your time and do the things right. Oyekun is to never think you know more then the forces. It is one of adhering to the rules and hierarchy of divinities, spiritual, and physical (natural) worlds. Know your position, your role, and perform your duties as expected. It is an oracle of supporting and expansion of family. Know that your actions can benefit, as well as, hurt others, especially family. Oyekun is to live long if you take good care of yourself; as it is to live short if you do not. Try not to do things alone, and don't be cheap – especially with divinities. The more you give them, the more you will receive from them.

**Example Tosses –
Read from Closest to Farthest – Top to Bottom**

First Toss - Itawa – Otura

1
0
1
1

2nd Toss - Eyeife - Ofun

$$0$$
$$1$$
$$0$$
$$1$$

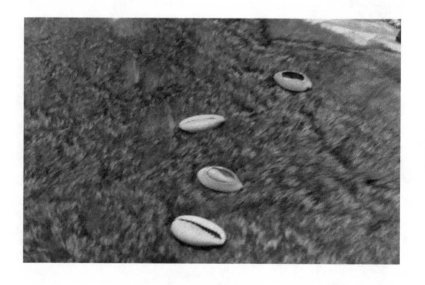

3rd Toss - Okana Sodde - Ika

0
1
0
0

All Tosses - 1011 - 0101 – 0100

0	0	1
1	1	0
0	0	1
0	1	1

All 16 signs

Part 2 Spiritual Remedies

Where Spiritual Connectivity Begins

At Home Spiritual Development

Before anyone can even conceptualize what connecting to a divinity might be, one needs to learn how to connect to pure spirituality. Pure spirituality is the universal energy which makes all things possible. It is the conscious will by which all things are made possible, or just God. Yet, this is the God force which is in the air, whether you call it energies without bodies, electromagnetic living particles, Star Wars (Midi-chlorians), psychic energy, or the spirit world. It becomes an enlightened base attained through dedicated, and devoted to solemn prayer for a very long time. This first connection is your vibration to all other forces which pick up your spiritual frequency.

I mention a long time, because this is not something you pick up one day, and put down the next, because of not hitting the mark on spiritual connectivity right away. You probably do not even know how it could or should work for you. Divinities are not just going to connect to you without posing challenges. These challenges are relative to proving yourself worth for them to even pay attention to you. You must be a good person; give your heart, and let go of the self. The connection requires many weeks, months, and even years of solemn spiritual meditation through prayers or mantras. When first started during my 20's, I found that my voice needed to resonate vibrations in the air. The echo of words denoted spiritual contextual meaning transcending barriers of physical walls, conscious and subconscious planes. Who is to say it does not go even beyond the stratosphere? My house had to literally feel like a

79

monastery. In other words, I read out loud.

It all begins with a simple home shrine. The shrine has to possess trinkets or ornaments which hold some sort of spiritual value to you. Some could be various small saints' statues, Buddha statues, candelabrum, Kabbalistic symbols, Crucifixes, pictures of deceased relatives, incense, flower vases, a Bible, pyramid, cologne, Florida Water, oils, and other spiritual essences. Light spiritual music can be playing in the background, if it is a way of getting into a spiritual mode. There needs to be a lit candle, at least 3 to 7 glasses of water, and books of prayers. An individual should dedicate at least 1 hour, 1 day per week for at least 2 years. During those 2 years, they are to pray for understanding of who they are, what is their mission here on Earth, and what have they come to accomplish in this lifetime. Pray for establishing a connection with spirit guides, and ancestors. Pray to have your 3rd eye opened for seeing and hearing what is readily not seen or heard by others. Your senses need to be opened to those divinities that have a message for your well being, and better good. Also, pray to be immune to danger, or see it before it arrives in order to escape danger. But, most of all, so that your connection to God and his forces become true, honest, and pure; that you are to be trusted by God's divinities for them to work with and through you.

Pure spirituality then gives rise to the materialization of spirituality. When one's contact has been made, what are you to do? How do you talk to it/them, or share a dialogue via communication system for understanding and verifying messages. This is the next stage, divination.

Prerequisites Before Beginning Remedy Work

1. Setting Up a Spiritual Altar

2. Generating a Spiritual Bath

3. Knowing How to Influence People Using Spirituality

4. Know How to Perform an Exorcism Using Ashes

1. Setting Up a Spiritual Altar - Spiritualism at Home, The Fundamental Principles of Santeria

Spiritual Presences on Shrine or Altar - Spiritual Understanding

Acknowledging Spirituality

Spirituality is that which binds all that is of existence in the universe, nature and us on Earth. We all have, and in a form of sense perception, instinct, intuition, spiritual abilities, a soul. We nurture the soul to develop strong spiritual abilities, through devotion with dedication to God or, that which is of God.

We believe that all that is of God is spiritual, seen or unseen. What is unseen begins as such until it can materialize into a form as matter. Yet, there are unseen molecules or particles present in the air, or water, unseen to the naked eye; which are already in their materialized form. Henceforth, there is always something. And, in the nothingness of something, is God. Do you remember hearing from your parents when as a child asking the question "mommy/daddy where is God?" and the answer always seems to be "God is everywhere, and in everything." Henceforth, spirituality is everywhere, as in connecting to God, is everywhere.

Human beings as walking, breathing, seeing and all sensing materialized spirits/souls.

We generate energy which is seen and unseen. We are made up of four distinct selves, melded together as oneself. These are the Physical Self, Emotional, Psychological, and last but not least, the Spiritual Self. This basic understanding can lead us to conclude that everything occurs to us in four ways as well as four times. For example, if by chance we were to get hit by a baseball. There would be the physical occurrence, trauma, consequence and reaction to being hit; a psychological impact/trauma of being hit; the emotional reaction of being hit; and the spiritual consequences, an event, tied to being hit. This simple rule can be applied to any traumatic or non-traumatic event in a person's life. Because of this spiritual tie, systems of divination and oracles, can tap in. There is also a network of spirits that communicate the event or what has transpired, as in a spiritual scribe or log that is taken down for each individual. Yet, that is another subject. For now, understanding that in order to resolve issues, occurrences, we should not to forsake a resolution at the spiritual level, as well. All healing or resolutions are not complete until a spiritual healing therapy solution is applied as well.

Spiritual Influenza

Spiritual consequences due to events that transpire in our lives can be classified as either positive or negative. Even though not all causes & effects are negative. There are negatives that turn to positive as in "sometimes we have to

84

lose to win." Having a spiritual occurrence or event can be said to be "spiritually influenced," as in acquiring an influenza that is in the air. What I am trying to say is that we humans generate positive or negative influenza, as a result of our actions and reactions. We attach influenza to one another no differently that we do a cold, virus, or flu. We assimilate or absorb this influenza as simple as by way of earth, wind, fire or water. Earth is by touching one another or surface; Wind is by molecules or dust particles that are in the air; Water is by touch or ingesting a fluid substance; Fire is through religious, spiritual, or fraternal political, ritual. Once an influenza is ascertained or acquired, what does one do? Well, apply a spiritual healing therapy solution. Spiritual healing therapy solution is a fancy way of saying voodoo ritual, spiritual cleansing, or holistic/alternative new age healing method. This normally involves the expunging or expulsion of negative energy through ritual.

There are many systems of spiritual relief or therapy out there for those who search. We suggest that you find what works for you. It does not matter of what denomination or religious belief or concept, there will always be a benefit. For those who want to experiment, venture out, and attempt to tap into the spiritual on their own, there is natural spiritualism.

Spiritual Devotion at Home:

Spiritualism, spiritual self-development, enlightenment, and enrichment on your own is a form of connection to God or the divine will of existence that is self acknowledged in all of us, even though family upbringing in a religious faith serves as a base. There are times where we search or want a little bit more. Now, let us take whatever spiritual base you have or do not have, and let us elevate it or expand it bit. This is done by erecting a sort of altar or shrine in your home. In no way is this worshipping of idols. For those who have a conflict with this idea, you will soon understand as you read; that it is not.

Let us start with your temple, holy land, comfort zone, which is your home. In most primitive cultures connecting to the divine begins in your first place of worship which is the home. The dwelling carries the family energy, vibe, spirituality, aura, essence, or glow. Each person's presence has a separate spirituality in itself, complex, vulnerable, susceptible, and reactionary. Each individual is a spirit, soul, presence, exhorting energy influencing things around them; made of internal and external forces, accompanied by spiritual energies. They can be called, Angel, Deity, entity, spiritual force, Saint, or spiritual protection. Then there are also our ancestors or past relatives. These link us to the divine, and we can relate them to being closest to God in the land of spirit or spirit world. Who is to say that their new task once in the land of spirit is not to look after those they left behind and protect them? I certainly wish so. For who is better than someone I knew and loved in flesh and blood, and loved me back, to look after me now. This form of spiritual understanding has been around for centuries and is very popular among Latinos. It is called Spiritualism, a

86

form of ancestral worship. Ancestor worship, as a divine link to God, can be viewed as paganism. Yet, what is the making of a Saint, the martyrs that died in the name of Jesus or Allah. Although Jesus converted Gentiles to Judaism; and from the conversions, Christianity was born. Who where the Gentiles? They were Pagans, and some worshipped ancestors. When we dedicate a religious service, mass or sermon in church to a relative that has traveled to the other side, what are we doing? We are honoring that spirit. We are acknowledging its existence or having existed. Venerating it, a praying to God that His heavenly Angels, accompany, protect, and give light and strength to this ancestor; so that its protection and blessing can be bestowed upon us as well by the Angels of God that walks with it.

Connecting to the spirit world or the divine from home, also involves connecting to spirituality outside our homes. God's universe is so vast and expansive, that we cannot fail to omit nature that is around us: the natural forces at play here, in which we are also vulnerable, susceptible to, and have battles with. We can connect to these forces from the comfort of our home in order to receive blessings and overt tragedies. With spirituality at our grasp, we can link to all that is at our disposition. So we are taught, made to believe or intuitively know. Getting all this out of the way, we can now focus on finding a special place in our home in which we can connect to the most divine.

Spiritual Altar or Shrine

This area of holiness does not have to be large. It is just a section, corner, or space, where you can set up a place for prayer, meditation, or solitude. Included in this space is a table, bookcase, or shelves, covered with white cloth. Whatever type of material that appeals to the individual is fine. Floor mats; a European, African or Persian rug for the floor. A stool, bench or chair to sit on, can also be included. Now, place three to seven clear glasses or wine glasses of water on the surface along with religious relics, statues, or icon, which will connect to your particular system of belief. For example; Catholic Saint, Divinity of Buddha, Hebrew Star of David, Hindu, Islamic, African Deity, or Native Indian symbols, etc. On this special table can also be added pictures of deceased relatives to serve as connections to ancestors. These figures represent what we are made up of or a part of. Now, we have what we can call a Shrine or Spiritual Altar.

Your, unique spiritual shrine can now be a place for channeling spiritual energy and focus. Bless this area by sitting and praying, lighting candles, burning incense, sprinkling holy water. Place offerings of food, fruit, and pastries, things that you like to eat on your shrine. You see, in the old days, part of acknowledging and honoring spiritual forces and divinities included giving – a giving/sacrificing to them. As in, "give onto those/others so that those/others give onto you." "He whom gives shall also receive." These phrases do not just apply to man giving to man. We believe they also extend to the forces around us that God has created. I guess this is one of those forgotten lessons, that in our times we fail to apply. He who gives to the spirits, nature, divinities, etc. will receive from them.

Have you ever heard the phrase "The Lord giveth, and the Lord taketh." Most of the time I have heard people use it when they lose something that is dear or of value to them. Yet, I don't believe the Lord takes; we just don't give enough in the form of servitude. And, if nature decides to take, it is because we have forgotten to give onto to nature willingly. Folks today have a way of thinking that God and his divine forces exist to work or serve them. When in actuality, we should work together, to serve God his divinities, and respect nature. When you do good, and do not look at whom you do good too, you will always receive goodness.

By the way, do not leave your offerings on your Shrines to long. It should always remain clean and free of stale food. With the devotion, dedication, humility, and righteous heart, the growth of your spirituality will bring great achievements and success.

Why? Waters, Herbs, & Candles:

Very simply, waters, herbs, & candles are spiritual conduits, which connect to the sublime forces of Heaven, Earth, and Spirit. These substances form the base for connecting and utilizing the basic fundamental elements Earth, Wind, Fire, & Water, in spiritual ritual. All that we can feel, see, touch, or smell that is manifest and materializes in one of these basic forms. All that is of nature carries these basic four spiritual elements within. Take man for instance, the body is three quarters water, the bones serve as dirt/earth, we breathe and expel gas/air/carbon, and we have energy generating heat. This can also be said about every living creature which God has created/generated through natural occurrence. As previously stated, everything is somehow connected. The Air we breathe is the electrical and gaseous carrier of molecules which everything that is of life absorbs. We are all connected to one another as simply as acknowledging that we breathe each others' air. What are sound waves, but electrical currents? What are colds, but parasitic infectious viruses when absorbed? Water, the secretion of such, is the plasma for generating or regeneration of organism, organic living tissue. Fire/Heat radiation from the Sun is the fusion for binding life, for growth and expansion, hence connects or awakens spirituality. Finally Earth, the ground, construct, frame, arena, realm, where things manifest as we know it. Earth is the outcome of the great manifestation of spirituality. Earth transmitted through the air has a form it is called dust. So, if we can positively charge dust we can neutralize negatively charged dust. The same can be said for water, air, and fire. There is a religious system which specializes, in spiritual therapy by positively charging and neutralization of negative, dust, air, earth, and water. It is Santeria. Believe it or not, the quasi-scientific principles outlined here, form a base understanding for fundamentals in the learning and connecting to spirit via Santeria. Santeria is all that is of an indigenous pagan culture connected via indoctrination to Christianity. It is the semi-copulation of two systems, on certain ideology, yet not on ritual. In Cuba it is the respect the enslaved Africans had for the masters, by allowing assimilation to their Christian ways, yet not forsaking the African indigenous religious concepts, rituals, and philosophy. The same can be said of Mexican, Venezuelan, Colombian, and Honduran Santeria; but from an Indigenous Indian spiritual realm, with

Christian connectivity. See how broad and expansive it can be.

Now, back to the herbs, candles, and waters (rose, sandalwood, colognes, holy etc.). To simplify, all this, we can venture to say herbs, roots, seeds, and minerals, with their medicinal, nutritional, and spiritual properties; combined or otherwise put through some form of fusion, whether spiritual or scientific are made into oils, candles, and powders. When dispersed in the air, absorbed, or ingested with water form and stimulate spiritual activity within and around us. Powders made from herbs, roots, seeds, or minerals carry medicinal properties to nourish, cure, heal, make ill or cause death; and can be dispersed in the air.

In conclusion, we can influence positive or negative change in our lives knowing how to work, spiritually with these substances. When you put all this together, we are offering these substances to spirits/spirituality which bless, charge, or activate it; and spiritual work has been done. In the giving, we are sacrificing, not taking for ourselves yet letting go. In this there is power too; for we are not giving to this world, utilizing for ourselves; but to the others in order to gain consideration, and recognition. The Spirits, Angels, Ancestor, Divinities, Deities or Forces/Spiritual Protections, respond or show there gratitude in the proof that we resolve the problem for which we performed ritual for.

The Weekly or Bi-Weekly Routine

Start with sitting down at your altar, once a week. Pick a day and time. Change the water in the glasses; replace flowers, oils, perfumes, candles etc. You are in essence refreshing your shrine. This is so that every week your life is refreshed and renewed. Read prayer books at your shrine or altar, light your candle, burn your incense. And, I believe you will see results, on how you can influence a positive change in your life.

Spiritual therapy can be applied and administered to the self at home. Since, you now have a basic concept, with consistency, devotion and dedication, results are assured. There are no rules for how long to apply your therapy. There is not an exact day or time for spiritual consideration. God, the divinities, and nature are not keepers of time as we are. There is no distance, space, or time restrictions for spirituality to reach, or work. It is the way it is, and we should accept how nature or spirituality manifests itself. For, further development in spiritual awareness, seek advice. Research, and learn with an opened mind. Yet, take care of not being coerced, or used. Everything, told has to make sense, and prices for spiritual work as donations should be made fair. By the way, when lighting a candle, know to whom, as a spirit or divinity, you are lighting it to; and for what purpose or reason. Make sure you state this, in your prayers. This is only a humble start in exploring the nature of spirituality. All things done with respect, humility, and responsibility will always be honorable.

There are many people buying books on candles; oils; herbal magic and spells; developing psychic abilities; and connecting to the spirit world. For those that do, I hope this sheds some light on the understanding that a place for all this work must be put together and maintained. In this way you are organizing spirituality, and not doing things without some knowledge, thought, structure, principle, or place of work.

How to Set-up a Spiritual Altar

You will need a small table (glass, wooden, wicker etc.) to your liking; 3 or 7 clear glasses (for water); a white cloth to cover the table; a vase for some flowers from time to time; some prayer books (Bible/ Book of Psalms/ Kabbalah/ Koran/ Hindu/ Buddhist). Most Spiritual stores carry them; I recommend one called "Selected Prayers"; it seems universal. I also wrote a book entitled, *Selection of Prayers for Enlightenment*, which provides a selection of prayers that one can use for their spiritual and meditative practice. Then, add pictures of desceased relatives and any statues or ornaments that express your spiritual consciousness. Finally, a 7-day white candle.

First, find a small area or corner of your home, be it the living room, dining room, home office; someplace where you will feel comfortable setting up a shrine. Start with a small table and white cloth on top of it. The table does not have to take up the whole space. Place on top of the table 3 or 7 clear glasses of water, a vase with flowers, a large 7-day white candle. Place pictures of the desceased relatives, especially those dearest to you. You can add to this table any other spiritual paraphernalia such as a Cross, Star of

David, African Statue, or Chinese Buddha; whatever has spiritual significant value to you and conveys your spiritual expression/ belief. If none, then none. Now, place a plate of food on this table as an offering to your spirituality and ancestors. Light the candle, and pray to God and your Ancestors to deliver you from any and all attacks, using your prayer book or books. It is good to dedicate about a half-hour to 45 minutes to these prayers/contemplation/ meditation.

This is followed up once a week, changing the water in the glasses and flowers, of course. The food can be thrown to the garbage the next day. When first initiating your altar, you should consistently do your prayers every day for 9 days, changing the plate of food every day. Then follow it up once a week. Once you open the communication you should keep it strong and connected, hence the advice of following up once a week.

2. Generating Spiritual Healing Herbs & Baths

Through prayers, burning incense, lighting candles, placing food/libation to the forces we nourish them, and they are satisfied. When we satisfy forces, or energies around us, the negative ones are appeased, and leave us alone. The positive ones are appeased and help us acquire blessings or maintain the blessing we already have. Negative energies, not only do they obstruct progress, they multiply and hang around until they are removed. Persons can have a multitude of negative traumatic events in their lives and carry the negative spirituality of them for many years; all because they have never addressed them spiritually, nor resolved them with a healing therapy treatment. Reoccurrences, even in a different style, are proof of what I am mentioning here. These negativities hang around, waiting for an opportunity to hurt again. Some examples of them are depression, animosity, curse, betrayal, envy, jealousy, bigotry, gossip, aggression, assault, loss, misery, necessity, suffering, justice situations, divorce, bad debts, bad luck, and heart break, just to name a few. Notice, how I have had not even mentioned witchcraft. In IFA Ideology, if a word denotes energy that can affect you, then it is a spirituality or force. When negative, the spiritual force is attributed to the category of arbitrary forces of affliction, decomposition, illness; or disease, as in, you are not well.

Good health (a divine treasure), obtaining a better paying job, a raise in your current one, falling in love, getting married, buying a house, having a child, not being indebted, being able to afford the finer things of life: Who does not like the good stuff, blessings umm, I can savor them, wish for them, and cannot wait for them; and how come they do not last? Obstructions, that's why. Obstacles, and intrusions, they come and you have to make them go. Negative influences too, are like a roulette wheel spinning until they land on someone. Some are even channeled towards you as is witchcraft, evil spells, hexes, or curses. Yet, others are just attributed to conditions set by the way we choose live, i.e. choices that we make which put us in predicaments. So you think and live, so you are. Then, there are the out-of-the-blue negativities, like a getting a ticket, fender benders, domestic quarrels which escalated. Minor negatives are the everyday bumps, bruises, colds, or flu's. Yet, those small ones do accumulate and turn into larger ones; so one has to treat those as well.

All these things, which have been pointed out, can be identified via divination. Granted, unless it is so obvious that you do not need divination. Yet, it is something good to have performed from time to time as a measuring tool. The importance of divination is to outline the negatives, so that you can apply the healing therapies to them. Outline, the positives so that you can apply spiritual work to secure the positive, or maintain it if you are already experiencing a positive way of being. Just note, that if you try divination on your own, although it will be something that you try by reading simple instructions from a book, it will take years of devotion to spirituality; living the prophecy of your divination, gaining experience acting upon, and practicing the solutions to the divination, that will eventually make you proficient. Being proficient requires a lifestyle change, and acquiring the respect, and merit of divine spiritual forces' support; and this comes through years of dedication called sacrifice. You may want to obtain divination from a professional shaman, IFA/Orisha priest, medium, psychic, tarot reader, or guru at first. The proof is in the pudding. From divination to prescribed spiritual healing therapy solution work, with the qualified professional, all spiritual work has to have a positive end result, a positive change for the better, in some way, form, or fashion. There are individuals, which have so much baggage that they need various sessions of spiritual cleanings and rituals in order to get rid of what has been accumulated through the years. Everyone is a bit different, and thus becomes a unique exception, even if having lived similar life traumas. Yet, that is for the experienced diviner or spiritual worker to ascertain. There is no way of measuring how much of a blessing is to be obtained from spiritual work. There are times where we make leaps and bounds, and other times when we just scratch surfaces. Nevertheless, we have had to notice a change, and most of the time it begins with an overwhelming feeling of weight being lifted off our shoulders, and a strong desire to sleep, or rest. Through rest comes stress relief, then the clear headiness to make good decisions.

Expulsion or expunging by way of incense is very common. Sage, bay leaf, garlic skins are but a few herbal substances, which can be used burn away simple negative energies. It is because of their known spiritual properties of fighting negative energies, which has been pasted down through the ages, within spiritual occult channels. Another form of cleansing is through spiritual herbal baths, or non-herbal. A non-herbal is one where we use different types of waters mixed. For example a combination including church holy water, rose water, orange blossom water, gardenia, and Florida water cologne; poured over your body, saying a prayer for purification. Another can be done in nature or

97

outdoors, on the beach, river, or lake. You start by first making an offering to the spirituality, divinity, or angel in charge of the position in nature, out of respect. It is a humble offering gesture of dried fruit, mixed nuts, or some coins. Then while in the water, you pour honey or molasses all over your body, then wash and rinse your body with nature's water. Then, continue enjoying yourself at your outing. All angels, divinities, Orishas, or divine forces have their position in nature. They serve and protect that position. That position is attributed to the divine force itself, and becomes a symbol of the divine force. As in, Our Lady of Charity (Oshun), being the guardian goddess of the rivers, St. Christopher (Agayu), being the guardian and representative of a volcanic mountain. When praying to them in their outdoor environment, bring a humble offering (without littering of course), acknowledge them share with them, and show respect. They will acknowledge you as well, and separate those who know, from those who do not too.

Spiritual herbal baths can be generated knowing the spiritual significance or property of a plant or herb. Plants or herbs are of most importance because of their medicinal as well, as nutritional values. When tasting an herb or spice, can you feel its astringent, sour, repugnant, sweet, salty, hot, refreshed, aromatic, properties? They can support healing, and make you sick. As in, used for positive or negative reasons. Herbs, whether ingested in a tea, or poured over our bodies, will support a change in mood enhance certain feelings, and attitude in that instance or moment in time.

When lighting a candle, and burning incense, please pray to a divine force, Orisha, or angel of your devotion for good things. Please, ask them from the heart, to help you overcome, and vanquish depression, anxiety, illness, or whatever ails you. When placing an offering of fruit or food. Ask that the negative energies of pain, suffering, loss, illness, whichever you feel is robbing or stealing your energy to be satisfied with your free will offering, and leave your body and environment. This is what is meant by applying a spiritual healing therapy solution by utilizing your altar/shrine. Positive changes will come, and many blessings too.

How to use Herbs & Spices for a Divine Spiritual Experience:

There is no special number of combinations of herbs or spices to use. A list of plants/herbs and spices, have been included in order to provide a wide range to choose from. Also, the herbs and spices listed can mostly be bought at the supermarket, at the fresh or dried spices section of your grocery store.

Grocery Store Herbs List

Name of Herb or Spice	Effects	Use
Allspice	Pain Relief	External/Internal
Aloe	Healing, Restores Cells	External/Internal
Angelica	Repellent, Against Evil	External/Internal
Anise	Love, Money, Attraction, Stimulant	External/Internal
Balm	Healing, Tranquilizing	External/Internal
Basil	All Purpose	External/Internal
Bay Leaf	Repellent, Healing, Anti-bacterial	External/Internal
Burdock	Repellent, Healing Anti-bacterial	External/Internal
Catnip	All Purpose	External/Internal
Chamomile	Repellent, Healing, Anti-bacterial	External/Internal
Chaparral	All Purpose	External/Internal
Cinnamon	Love, Money, Healing, Attraction	External/Internal
Cocoa	Healing, Lubrication, Soothing	External/Internal
Cilantro	Love, Money, Healing, Attraction	External/Internal
Dandelion	All Purpose	External/Internal
Echinacea	Repellent, Healing, Against Evil	External/Internal
Eucalyptus	Repellent, Healing, Against Evil	External/Internal
Fennel	Repellent, Healing, Against Evil	External/Internal
Garlic	Repellent, Healing, Against Evil	External/Internal

100

Ginger	All Purpose	External/Internal
Ginkgo	Healing, Anti-Aging	External/Internal
Ginseng	Health Restoration, Stimulant	External/Internal
Hops	Healing, Tranquilizer	External/Internal
Hyssop	Love, Money, Healing, Stimulant	External/Internal
Kola	Love, Money, Healing, Stimulate	External/Internal
Majoram	Love, Money, Healing, Attraction	External/Internal
Mint	Love, Money, Healing, Attraction	External/Internal
Motherwort	Healing, Tranquilizer	External/Internal
Myrrh	Repellent, Cleanser, Against Evil	External/Internal
Oregano	Repellent, Healing, Attraction, Against Evil	External/Internal
Parsley	Luck, Healing, Attraction, Against Evil	External/Internal
Passion Flower	Healing, Tranquilizing	External/Internal
Pennyroyal	Repellent, Healing, Against Evil	External/Internal
Red Clover	Repellent, Healing, Against Evil	External/Internal
Rosemary	Love, Money, Healing, Attraction	External/Internal
Saffron	Love, Money, Healing, Attraction	External/Internal
Sage	Repellent, Healing, Against Evil	External/Internal
Thyme	Repellent, Healing, Against Evil	External/Internal
Valerian	All Purpose	External/Internal

Spiritual Baths Preparation:

When herbs are fresh, run through the blender or food processor with plenty of water. When herbs are dry, boil along with seeds and stems or added spices. After having created the tea like substance let cool, and pour into a bucket or large bowl; add more water, honey and fragrance. Make enough to fill a gallon. Store gallon in refrigerator, and use everyday until finished. Another way is to split the Bath into 3 parts for 3-day use. When ready to use, pour the bathwater into a large bowl or plastic container, take to the shower, add warm water from the shower, after bathing just before stepping out. Then, there is the adding of the spiritual bath to the filled tub water to soak and bathe in it. Then, one just towel dries.

Always remember to pray over your bath, when generating it, and while applying the bath, in which manner you have chosen. Use prayers in your accustomed, religious denomination and language. You can light a candle, and burn some incense in the bathroom too. This will definitely enhance the experience, and create an aromatic therapeutic event.

Love & Money Attraction Bath:

Buy and use these herbs, or spices; Anise, Basil, Cinnamon, Cilantro, Ginger, Hyssop, Kola, Marjoram, all sweet Mints, Rosemary, and Saffron. Once boiled add, honey, cologne or personal fragrance preferred.

Cast Away Evil or Jinx Removal Bath:

Buy and use these herbs, or spices; Angelica, Bay, Chaparral, Echinacea, Eucalyptus, Fennel, Garlic, Myrrh, Oregano, Parsley, and Sage. No fragrance. Just add; white rum, palm oil, and cascarilla (peace powder).

Health or Wellness Bath:

Buy & use these herbs; Allspice, Aloe, Angelica, Basil, Chamomile, Cocoa, Dandelion, Garlic, Pennyroyal, Red Clover, Sage, Thyme, & Valerian. Can be used with a fragrance, in combination with white rum, and cascarilla (peace powder).

Teas for ingesting can be made from most of these herbs. Check the list above, to see which one says internal as well as external. Make a tea add whatever you would like to taste. Research, the medicinal properties of the herb, and most important know if you have any allergic reaction to one of them. If so, do not use it.

Note: please be mindful of what not to, use that can cause an allergic reaction to you. The list of herbs mentioned here are found in most grocery stores, or herbal specialty stores. They should not pose any threat. Yet, like all things, know your body. Like with all herbal medicines, please consult your physician before ingesting; do your homework. Not all on this list have to be used at the same time; use any combination that works with your system and taste.

Some Orisha Plants

There is a very huge variety of plants used in Orisha worship. These plants are not made readily available in all towns nationwide. Specially, if there are no Cuban botanicas around. This is why I had decided to utilize the grocery store herbs concept. They are readily available. Yet, I had compiled some Orisha herbs most popularly used, some time ago. If one were to see a Lucumi shaman and needs ritual work with herbs, they will send you to a "Botanica" pronounced (Bo-ta-nee-ka), and most likely they will tell you the name of the plant; by what it is known as within the Lucumi society.

3. How to Influence People Using Spiritualism

Once an individual is on the path towards elevating spiritual consciousness through practice and devotion to what they believe in, there are certain rules and regulations to follow and obey. Staying focused on growth and consistency in practice; their spirituality, grace, and gift will grow.

The individual will begin to acknowledge a positive change in their destiny. According to Ifa, destiny is what we ordinarily live day to day and how we manifest ourselves daily. To have a positive destiny is to not have obstacles or negative occurrences frequently. An individual should be able to look back throughout the year and honestly say that he/she has had more normal and good moments than bad moments. This is what meant by a positive destiny.

There are everyday occurrences that are part of life and are supposed to happen for experiences are made of these occurrences whether positive or negative; and we are to learn from them. This is part of how wisdom is achieved. Things cannot always go our way. Yet, when things just do not seem to go right, and go from bad to worse, we need to take action. Taking action is not just in a physical, emotional, or psychological form; these are easier. Folks forsake an even trouble-free form of taking action: Spiritual action.

Spiritual action will complement and enhance the other three courses of action. At times, until one has applied a spiritual solution to the problem, an occurrence will not go away. The negative influence becomes impeded in the person's karma, and hopefully, the person will not get used to it to the point of feeling that life for them is always going to be this way. Well, bad things are not supposed to re-occur. When they reoccur it means we have never gotten rid of the spiritual trauma generated by the sequence of events which transpired in our lives.

Be it in a past, present, or re-occurring future, spiritual cleansing is a way of expunging negative influences. Most people sage their homes, and themselves. There are many more forms of cleansing out there; a visit to a trained professional spiritual healer can divulge more of what I am talking about. For now, I am focusing on folks' understanding on how to help themselves and how to utilize a spiritual altar. For true heavy voodoo spells/work, strong cleansing, and offerings to divinities on shrines involving rituals, it is best left to the initiated priest or priestess who have undergo the required training, apprenticeship, responsibility, and sacrifice. And until one is ready to dedicate fully, it is not wise to get involved in those heavy works mentioned above. The spiritual altar is simple, it is universal, and does not pose a threat to one's person, spirituality, and karma. If one does not go to the dark side a spiritual altar should be ok. Spiritual baths with herbs for expulsion of negative energies will be dealt with in another article.

One of the first spiritual acts for generating spiritual activity or involvement is through prayer. Prayer is powerful because it is the channeling of the thought and breath via incantation. We can change the air with the sound waves of our voices, through calling out to the forces to influence change for the meaning in which the prayer is being recited. How far does air travel? How far can our voices carry a message? How far does smoke actually travel, any kind of smoke, cigar, cigarette, carbon monoxide, or from a charcoal barbecue. How far does smoke travel to reach our ozone, or stratosphere, and atmosphere? Who is to say that the winds will not carry our voices and breath/smoke clear across the other side of our world? Can you visualize this? This is one of the reasons I say that spirituality has no distance, space, or time. If a person can pray for evil from far away, a person can pray for good from far away. Can we write a prayer, or desire, with a person's name on a piece of paper, and burn that paper then cast its ashes to the wind? How far will the last molecule or dust particles rise, and fly across to whom our message is intended?

When studying philosophy, I will never forget the first philosophical question that was posed and answered. Is there a God? The answer was, if we are possible God is possible, anything is possible. The Yoruba concept of Oree, as the spiritual head of an individual connected to their soul, also serves as spiritual antenna. In other words your energy field has an antenna, which picks up transmissions. Some people just know or feel this; others do not seem to have a clue. Believe it or not, people who do not believe are much easier to be influenced than those who do because they would never believe things work this way and especially on them.

Now, the basis for channeling or invoking a spell is to generate a change or influence a change. Hopefully, most people who would do this can do so for a righteous cause. But we all know what can be done/used for good intentions can also be turned/used for bad intent. I pray that more folks learn to do positive spiritual work to help themselves or others than negative. Yet, it is when it is left to one's own responsibility; consequences do occur as a result; and what goes around will come around. Persons who do evil will receive evil, for the evil never left them. The author of an evil act is to whom the evil belongs. The person channeled what is theirs and shared it. The person receiving the evil, when removing it through a spiritual healing ritual, will release it. The part of evil which was shared, returns, or is re-acquired, hence, the boomerang effect.

Spiritual acts for imposing one's will upon others may work for a little while, yet the spells, like all things, disintegrate, decompose, or run out of gas. All spells need to be re-charged or nourished. Also, individuals have a Spiritual Guardian or Guardian Angel and spiritual protections, and ancestors; we are not alone. These spirit guides will eventually try to inform the individual that something is wrong. If the person has a form of communication, is spiritually endowed, or seek advice or help, he/she will find out.

Who would want to live trying to dominate people, or resorting to spells to control others all the time? This is no way to live. These people after a while forsake the positive channeling which would lead them to acquire what they need in the eyes of God anyway. There is an Oracle of Ifa which teaches us that we need to pray to God and his divinities not for what we want or desire but to pray for what we need. In this way, we allow God and his divinities the opportunity to surprise us. This act will bring to our lives something better than what we could have imagined or asked for. Yet, little spells that are done for a positive outcome and not for hurting anyone, just for love, or persuading are good. Or are they?

Channeling a spell to influence someone is easy. And if a person has a spiritual altar and has been dedicated to it for a while, its energy should be very strong. The connection established through dedication with the angels, deities, ancestors, or divinities that they have called upon has become a norm for both the person and the divinities. The forces have become accustomed to receiving spiritual energy from the offerings or gifts. Candle light, incense, fruits, sweets, food, all serve as energy for spiritual forces to nourish themselves. You might ask how a spirit can nourish itself from something that needs to be taken, eaten or absorbed. Well, the decomposition process of food expels gas. This gas rises to the air which now can come in contact with spirit. A life force without a body is one of the definitions for Spirit.

Candle light is important because divinities come toward the light. The light represents our conscious plane of reality or dimension, the belief of being seeing, to see, to bring to light. Also, when a candle is dedicated to let's say St. Michael, you are offering light to the idea of the existence, faith, and belief in St. Michael. The offering becomes a giving up of your light, forsaking light, as in sacrificing light that you would normally use for yourself away to St. Michael. This is an ancient thought because we no longer use candles for everyday lighting; unless it is an emergency we have electricity. Well, if you feel like forsaking electricity as an offering to St. Michael do so and see what you will receive from St. Michael. The Angel accepting/receiving your offering with compassion will return the gesture with a gift. This happens with us as well, when we receive a gift, we hope to be able to reciprocate it. When we light a candle, make an offering, please assign it to a known divinity, I am sure they will appreciate it, and give you proof of their existence. A sign will come, I am sure of it.

Finally, here is the spell for influencing someone or list of people. Let us begin with a scenario in which you are going to mediate over a lawsuit, where you would be the recipient of a large sum of money. Let us say that the company came with an offer, and in the bargaining process you are trying to get as much money as you can. Granted the company probably has a cap, and are going to try to settle for less than what your lawyer is asking. So, you would want to generate a spell on your altar to influence the company's lawyers and mediators to give in to your demand or reach as close to your amount as possible. First, you need to decide which divinity is going to backup or accept this spell or work. In order to do this you need to perform divination for yourself. You can use the Yoruba Lucumi 16 Oracle Geomancy, I-Ching, Tarot, Runes, etc. You need a system in which you can ask a yes or no question, one divinity at a time, till you hit upon the divinity that is going to accept the work. If you cannot perform divination for yourself call a spiritualist, medium, psychic, Yoruba priest, Wicca priestess, or Babalawo and have them ask the question for you. Once you have the name of the divinity. You would need to obtain a picture, candle, or image of this divinity, with a prayer to call upon it. On your altar, place a glass of water dedicated to this divinity and a candle. Write a petition on a piece of paper using a no.2 pencil stating the name of the divinity, the person or person's that need to be

110

influenced and for what reason; the for whom is, of course your name and your lawyers. Word it so that all negotiations are to go your way, in your favor. Place the petition inside a small glass or clear shot glass. Add honey, cinnamon powder, powdered Valerian root, mint, marjoram, and camphor water (camphor water can be purchased at a Spanish botanica or spiritual store it is normally also called sedative water, or agua sedative). You can also take some camphor put in water for ½ hour, and the water will become camphor water. You can also obtain the Valerian leaves or root at a natural herb store or vitamin shop. Valerian helps to calm as in making someone sleepy. When someone is sleepy, their guard is down. Scrape or crush some Valerian root into powder, if not already in powdered form. Use a very small amount, the essence of the herb is what is important, not the amount. Honey and cinnamon represent sweetness and heat; the spiritual energies needed for promoting love or good desires.

After mixing/making the spell, place the shot glass next to the items dedicated to the divinity and light the candle. This should be done at least 2 to 3 days before going to mediation. Remember everyday leading up to the mediation date, say the prayer, make your request to the divinity, and light the candle. The spell is then discarded after mediation, in the garbage until needed again if going to court, or second meeting. By the way, you can keep the shot glass, to be reused. This same spell can work for requesting a raise or going to see someone who owes you money, or to get someone to like you. It can be used to subdue tension around you, when people are quarrelsome, or have a negative attitude towards you.

111

You probably are asking why the spices of marjoram and mint. Well, they are sweet herbs. Herbs are normally used for flavoring foods, or our palette, our tongue. They also have spiritual properties, and serve the same purpose when used in a spell. "May their aroma and taste, sweeten the palette of the persons I need influenced, and are good and positive with me." Also, these herbs are readily available at a grocery store. I would not have you use Orisha/Santeria herbs that you would not be able to readily identify at a botanica.

4. Knowing How to Perform an Exorcism with Ashes

During these years of practicing the religion, I have come across situations that have challenged my knowledge and interpretation of religious ideological concepts. These situations have been moments where I have experienced the manifestation of divine grace (ashé), pronounced (ahshe), within me. They have been last moment incidents where I have been called upon to resolve a situation without prior notice or advance preparation. Such was a situation which occurred four years ago, which has stayed forever imbedded in my data bank of resolutions.

While working in the home of one of my godchildren in Queens, NY, I received a phone call from Miami where a friend of the family was going through a great ordeal. Her name was Sidka. She said to me "please help! Jose is going crazy! Something terrible is upon him! He is hurting himself! He wants to throw himself out of a window! We have him sedated!" Needless to say she was crying, frantically, and didn't know what to do; and did not want to call rescue or the police. As I calmed her down, my mind instantly zeroed in on what I knew of Jose. Jose was a gardener. A hard working man which owned a landscaping business, and apparently had clients with very large yards, whom had enemies. Instantly, what occurred to me was that he had stepped on some evil witchcraft in one of his clients' homes during work. I immediately took out my divination chain (okpele), and asked Ifa, if this was true and the answer was "yes". What most people do not know about Miami is that, it is very strong in positive and negative hoodoo. You would have had to live there in order to recognize it, know it and live through it. The party city, to most, is also a megatropolis of hoodoo voodoo (LOL). Just think of it. It is the gateway to the Caribbean, South, and Central Americas. There is not a neighborhood that does not have a spiritual store close by. Those coming from these regions have deposited their traditional practices, food, and culture in Miami. Establishing the fact that Jose's situation was negative spirituality (evil witchcraft) related. I automatically knew that he would have to be exorcized of this and soon, before he gets committed to a psycho ward. All of a sudden the thought of ash, armasigo, and cascarilla, came to mind. Immediately, I asked of Ifa, if with these three ingredients I can devise a healing therapy which would cast away the negativity that had befallen Jose. Bring to ease his affliction, and helping a distressed family from afar. Well, here goes the instant recommendation I suggested.

Boil some armasigo (gumble limbo) plant, leaves, or bush; add a little palm oil, generating a spiritual bath. Let cool, remove the plant and add white rum, aguardiente (fire water), or overproof rum. Make enough for two gallons or two baths. Obtain a cup of wood or charcoal ashes, and a cup of crushed cascarilla. The person needing the work done to them is to be stripped of all their clothing in the bath tub. Their face and whole body is to be powdered with the ashes, and the armasigo (gumble limbo) bath is to be poured over their head & body. They are to then shower or bathe as normal with soap and fresh water. The next day they are to repeat the procedure, yet this time they are to powder their face & body with crushed cascarilla, followed by the armasigo bath and regular shower.

Note: Cascarilla is peace powder chalk. It can be bought at any Cuban/Spanish botanica

A week later, I received a call directly from Jose expressing his gratitude and told me his version of the story. It was very funny as he explained it, we both laughed throughout his version of it. Specially the part where he mentioned something jumping off or out of him as his wife poured the first bath over him. Then, the second bath just reinforced the expulsion and brought him peace. He further explained that where he first started to feel funny was at a client's yard, where he knew that they had a shed in the back full of mysterious stuff. He apparently got to close to the shed or ran over something ill intended for his clients with the lawn mower or weed eater. The part of his story which was not funny, was where he mentioned having the overwhelming sensation of throwing himself in front of a truck. What really amazed me was that when I generated this particular healing therapy solution, it was intended to help him temporarily until I arrived in Miami a couple of days later, in order to work on him directly. There are much stronger rituals within the Ifa system of therapies which can be applied to this situation. Yet, it actually took care of his problem. He did not come visit me for a follow up reading and ritual cleansing until three months after.

This particular ceremony is not just for semi-extreme cases such as Jose's. It can also be for those that feel depression, anxiety, desperation; those who work in hospitals, or which have dangerous jobs, where they have witnessed the deaths of others. It is for anyone who has suffered traumatic situations which have not left them - all those feeling as if something dark is attached or latched on to their bodies,

115

those coming out of prison, or returning from war. Most folks are unaware of the negative energies which we pick up. These energies can be spirits or entities nourishing themselves with/of our darkness. When these negative spiritualities stay imbedded within us for a long time, they continually influence our darkness, not allowing our positive energies to take its turn in generating good things. Hence, we need help or support in casting them away.

Also note that this is a simple ceremony which can work on most. Yet, for stronger negative influences nothing beats a true exorcism. Now, in my book an exorcism does not only imply removal of diabolical entities. They are also applied for the same reasons that I mentioned above. Expulsion of negative energies which we have attained through traumatic incidents in our lives or cast upon us by way of channeled witchcraft. I perform such rituals and much more powerful ones on myself and others, just to remain positively focused. These rituals get rid of negative spirits or witchcraft. I get smacked every now in then just by being in spiritual wars' line of fire.

Many years ago while pondering on the thought of the following statement; "from ashes to ashes, dust to dust." I came to the understanding that ashes can be used to get rid of negative spirits. I guess because we do become dust all over again during our after death decomposition process. We become solvent fertilizer and nourishment for mother earth. Hence, the ground takes all that decomposes only to recycle it over again and give back in new growth or life. Ashes made from any organic substance which has been incinerated or put to fire signifies a return to earth. It sends a message to an entity or spirit that it has returned or should return to earth. As in "go back! and nourish the ground you came from!" Then, it leaves the premises. Ash is used in spiritual baths that we Babalawo's make for clients for these purposes as well as in teas for removal of ingested witchcraft. Ash is also a base ingredient in organic soap, so it has natural cleansing properties. The white chalk powdered egg shell (cascarilla) is one of the Religion's power substances. I always say "Never under estimate the power of an Egg." An egg is a simple representation of life force being generated. The whiteness of the shell is what the life is encased in; it is part of its spirituality and its protection. Henceforth, white powdered eggshell is a spiritual substance for countering or removal of darkness, blocking it, and generating peace.

The gumble limbo plant or also known as the rubber plant in some places, because of its rubbery sticky resin, has healing properties. Its tea can be used for treating some diseases and other ailments. It is one of our Yoruba Lucumi power plants of expunging negativity and healing. My great-grandma used this plant quite often, and in most of her healing therapy applications. I have always looked at it as having the power of making negativity bounce off of people (get it, rubber plant).

117

How to Perform an Exorcism with Ashes and Peace Powder

Ingredients: Ashes from 2 charcoal, 2 cascarilla (peace powder), Bayleaf (laurel), Basil (albaca), Rosemary (romero), Sage (salvia) and White rum; when unable to obtain the true herbs for this work, which are rompe saraguey, espanta muerto, quita maldicion, mar pacifico, armasigo, alamo, and vencedor.

Preparation: Boil the bay leaf, basil, rosemary, and sage in a big pot for 15 minutes. When done let cool, then strain into a bucket. Add the rum. Make enough bath for 2 days and crush enough ash and peace powder (cascarilla) for 2 days. Keep the ashes in a cup, and the powdered cascarilla in another.

On the first day:

Enter the bathroom and place a small candle on a corner of the tub. Bring the bucket of bath into the tub. Strip away all clothing. While naked powder your whole body with the ashes. Do a Lord's Prayer and ask in the name of God and the Holy Spirit that all negative spirits, spiritualities be expunged. Then pour the bath water over your body. Then shower normally as accustomed.

On the 2nd day:

The as above, yet this time powder your body with the cascarilla (peace powder). Then pour bath water over your head and body. Then shower normally as accustomed.

After the 2 days of cleansing - do the following for positive enrichment.

Mix coconut water, holy water, Florida water, egg white, and peace powder (cascarilla) in a bowl. Shampoo the solution rubbing and washing into your head, praying to release all darkness from your aura, and crown chakra. This releases tension, anxiety, depression, and should clear your mind. Repeat as many times as needed until you're relieved.

How to Overcome an Evil Spirit

Here is what you will need to do. Do you have a spiritual altar? If you do not then you need to set one up.

Then, I need you to generate a spiritual bath using herbs against evil. You will generate enough of the bath for 9 days.

You need to understand that your altar is a place for channeling spiritual energies, entities, and all spiritual forces.

I need you to understand this because you will need help from the spiritual forces that I want you to contact. These spiritual entities are going to take the place of a Babalawo/trained priest-ess not being there physically to expunge what you are going through. In other words, you need the help of spiritual forces to get rid of the one that is molesting you.

Now, that you have a spiritual alter or shrine. Now, that you have a cast-away evil bath for 9 days. I want you to find a prayer to the lost souls of purgatory and picture, if possible, at a spiritual store or internet; Animas Solas. I also need for you to find a picture and prayer of the Santisma Muerte, the Mexican Female grim reaper. What most people do not know is that these entities can be used for good, and to help you overcome other dark forces.

Once you have these pictures and prayers... you are to add a glass of water to your altar for each of these forces, Animas Solas and Santisma Muerte. You are to sit at your altar at a time when no one can bother you or interrupt you. You are to light a green candle to the Santisma Muerte, and a red to Animas Solas. Then dedicate a bowl of fruit on your altar for the Santisma Muerte, and vase with mixed flowers to Animas Solas.

For the next 9 days you to call on the Santisma Muerte & lost soul Animas Solas, for their support in expunging, expelling, and getting rid of this spirit that is molesting you. In the name of God the Father, Son, & Holy Spirit, with the support as well the hierarchy of Angels. That you are dedicating these prayers along with 9 Our Fathers, and Hail Mary's, in their honor, as they are honorable spirits of God... which are here for our use in order to overcome all evil, obstacles, negative human and spiritual forces, that rob us of our peace and harmony. That you are honoring them with the fruit for Santisma Muerte, and flowers to Animas Solas, as payment for the job done of getting rid of this spiritual enemy (mention the name of the spirit if you know it). If you do not know its name, you say, "spiritual enemy that is molesting me". You have the power to remove and get rid of it from my psyche, life, space, body, and house. So please do so. Mention that your body is the Lord's temple, and that no garbage can live in that which is holy to God, and that you consider yourself to be purified by them, the waters of the bath... then say 3 times "enemy of mine leave, enemy of the Santisima Muerte leave, enemy of Animas Solas leave. So it is said, so it is done, in the name of the Father, Son, Holy Spirit. Amen."

At the end of the 9 days you are to take the flowers and fruit to the cemetery and leave by a tree or abandoned tomb. When you return then perform this bath for the next 2 days.

After this you would have earned enough merit in the eyes of the Animas Solas, and Santisima Muerte to call on them again in the same way; yet for other situations, i.e. relationship problems to keep mate in line, for them to return, or for someone to leave you alone. You can call on them to get for a raise at work or finding a new mate, friend, or job. Call on them to help you control people or have people adhere to your needs. This is a very powerful spell, especially when you have the tools and have perfected channeling energies, spirits and forces. It all begins with an altar at least, or shrine.

Many blessings to you, may God bless you, and may these spiritual forces help you overcome what is haunting you.

Instructions for a Simple Ground Feeding Ritual

It is very important that folks every now and then give back to Earth. Mother Earth, Terra, the ground, from dust we come, dust we return; encompasses all the energies around us, ancestors, land of the dead, and rebirth. We stand on top of decomposed organic matter, along with minerals, quartz crystals, elements, and live organisms as well. Hence, we are feeding nature and all that is spiritually manifested by it, right then. Just like any of the other forces, out of acknowledgement, consideration, appreciation and respect; it will bless you in return (he that giveth, shall receive). This is done right in your backyard, for what better place than your dwelling, temple, spiritual abode, than the land where you live.

There are different levels of doing this of course, as in small productions, medium productions, and large productions. The medium and large production we will leave for the trained Yoruba priest or Babalawo to officiate. The small production includes 9 plates with different offerings, and they are:
1. Small pumpkin or squash
2. Whole small fresh fish (tilapia, snapper, or catfish)
3. One small steak
4. Bag of Pork Rinds
5. Bag of corn tortilla chips
6. Sugar
7. Coffee
8. Yam
9. 2 eggs

Aside, you will need rum, palm oil, honey, efun (cascarilla), Ori (shea or cocoa butter), roasted corn and smoke fish. You would need to know a simple Mojuba (Mo-you-ba) invocation prayer and how to toss the oracle of the 4 pieces of nut shells (coconut, Kola nut, or cowrie shells), for verification.

Instructions:

Go to the backyard and find an open place with room to open a hole about 1 foot deep, by 1 foot wide. Then bring all 9 plates and places in front of the hole, in a row, facing east. Add to the hole, the powdered smoked fish and jutia, roasted corn, a little palm oil, honey, rum, cascarilla, and shea butter. Have water in a bowl or gordy and the four coconuts (obi) in front of the hole. Proceed to invoke, pray or do mojuba. Direct yourself to Mother Earth, the land of the ancestors, and nature and the minerals. Explain why you opened the hole, and that you wish to feed her, her children, nature, ancestors, and the spirit world. Toss the coconuts to obtain acknowledgement. Then take the first plate which is pumpkin, present it to your head by lifting the plate and gently touching your forehead with it, then place the pumpkin or squash in the hole. Proceed with the fish, then the steak. These are the main ingredients which get presented to earth and by the person that is giving the offerings.

Now, all the others that are invited to be cleaned with the other offerings can proceed. The main individual is last, with the remainder of what is left on each plate.

Each individual is to take a hand full of the items, one item per plate. They can do two plates at a time. Hold the ingredients firmly in your hands without opening your

126

hands, and rub your body from head to toe. This symbolizes the ingredients in your hand absorbing your negative energy, then toss the ingredients in your hands to the hole, and proceed with the next two plates. Continue until the final plate which is the eggs. These are not to be broken or tossed in the hole by anyone except the person who is giving the ground feeding to begin with.... What everyone else does with the eggs is take an egg in each hand, then close your eyes, and gently rub your eyes with each egg, then place the eggs back on the plate. The last person is the person giving the offerings, hence, they rub their eyes then toss the eggs in the hole. When all has been offered to the ground, close the hole by filling it with dirt, using a small shovel, or whatever you used to open it. Add water on top of the hole, then place a small lit candle on top.

Basic Instructions for a Simple Door Feeding

The front door of a house needs to be fed at least 2 - 3 times a year. This is done to insure blessings and safety to all living in the home. To the Yorubas, all doors are portals, especially the front door of your dwelling. This is evident due to the difference between one realms feel, in relation to what you is felt crossing into another plane or realm. Example, when you are in your home with your doors closed, it is your plane or realm of existence; and as soon as you step aside you are in another realm of existence. Have you ever felt safety upon entering your home? Have you ever felt a sense of fear or paranoia upon stepping outside? Your space accumulates your positive energy, and you are not exposed to external forces or energies. Once outside we are vulnerable to external forces and energies.

There are two spiritualities which reside on every door or portal: the outer spirituality or outer door spirit, and the inner spirituality or inner door spirit. Both as a unified force are fed on the bottom door sill, metal, or tile, divider on which your door resides on top of, or stops. This is done along the length of the door. If, this door sill extends inside, you can feed inside. If the door sill extends outward you can feed outside. Nevertheless, both spiritualities share this door separator and they will both be satisfied. The outer door spirituality, in appreciation for acknowledgement and consideration, will gain the necessary strength to ward off dark forces, and keep the negative influences outside the door. The inside spirituality, in appreciation for acknowledgement and consideration, will allow for blessings to reach or enter the home. There are times when we are waiting for something positive to arrive. As in, waiting for an overdue raise, interviews for a new job and no calls. Money owed to us in from one source or another; it is there, yet not come through. Well, this simple ritual can aid in pulling in the blessing. Although this ritual is best done by a trained priest, I have created an extract from one of the many different ways in which the door energies are fed. For those reading this that are priest or priestess, black peas will represent (Ekru), the yellow cornmeal to represent (Eko). It is not all the time that the door energies need eyegbale.

Ingredients:

Glass of water, small white candle, palm oil, corn meal, 1 can of black eye peas, cocoa butter or shea butter, cascarilla (efun), honey, and rum. When a priest or priestess, powdered smoked fish & bush rat (jutia), 4 obi's (coconut pieces) for affirmation toss.

Instructions:

Take the can of black-eyed peas, place in a bowl, add 3 tablespoons of yellow corn meal, 1 teaspoon of palm oil, add a teaspoon of shea or cocoa butter, and some crushed cascarilla (efun), about 1 tablespoon of honey, and a swig of rum. If you are doing this in the bowl, using a fork or spoon crush and mix all the ingredients together, as in creating a thick paste.

Next, take the bowl with the mixture, glass of water, and candle to the front door of your home. Place the the glass of water and candle on a plate next to the door on the inside near the opening. If the door sill, metal or ceramic separator is on the outside. Open the door. If it is on the inside you can leave the door closed. Take some rum and pour along the length of the door. This is to awaken the door spirituality, then pour some water along the door separator. Add some palm oil, and honey too. Then, proceed to praying in a way accustomed to. If you are a practicing priest or priestess, toss obi for affirmation. Then, place the mixture all along the length of the door, on the bottom metal or tile threshold. Light the candle. After about two hours, pick up the offering, break up into 3 portions, and separate making 3 packages. Use brown bag paper. The final destination is to 3 four-corner crossroads.

If you have Eleggua, you can place him next to the glass of water and candles, and pour some of the mixture on him, including him and praying that he strengthens the door, brings blessings that have been denied to the house.

Spiritual Baths to Expunge Negative Influences and Attract Positive Influences

First Bath is to expunge negative influences.
Second Bath is to attract positive energies.

Bath #1
Ingredients:

Charcoal ash, powdered white egg shell, white rum, bay leaf, basil, sage, and parsley.

Instructions:

Boil the basil, bay leaf, sage, & parsley in a pot for about 15 mins. Let cool, remove the herbs, then add to the bath water a tablespoon of charcoal ash and crushed egg shell, then a shot of rum. Pour into a gallon jug and keep in the refrigerator for to be used 3 days in a row.

Use:

Pour two cups of the bath in another large wash pan, or bowl. Take to the shower. After you have taken your regular shower, place the bowl under the warm water of the shower to add a little more so that it is not so cold. Then, pour the bath all over your body. Do this for 3 days.

After the 3 days - Stop for a day then proceed with the next spiritual bath

Bath #2
Ingredients:

Basil, catnip, cinnamon, cilantro, ginger, hyssop, marjoram, mint/spearmint/peppermint, saffron, & rosemary; honey, rum, and colognes such as; violet, sandalwood, rosewater, orange blossom, & vetiver.

Use: two tablespoon of each herb - boil - then let cool - remove the herbs - then add honey, rum, and colognes - pour into a gallon jug - place in the refrigerator and pour a bath just like above for 5 days straight or until done

This treatment can be done once every 45 days.

Simple Love Spell

Take a piece of brown paper and write a petition on the paper with a No. 2 pencil like this, "Animas Solas, Pomba Gira, Santisima Muerte, may (name), desire me, love me, look for me, value, respect, can not resist, marry, and can not live without me. So it is said, so it is done".

Add a dab of honey and some cinnamon on top of the paper. Fold, and twine with a red string.

Place inside an empty can or glass bottle. Add sugar, cinnamon, and sweet red wine. Place on an altar or shrine, and cover it with a red cloth. Buy some flowers for your altar, and change the flowers every 5 days, dedicating the prayers and flowers to a different entity. Light the candle to the Animas Sola and do the prayer for 5 days. Then light a candle to Pomba Gira with prayer for 5 days. Then, finally to Santisima Muerte for the last 5 days. Then bury in the front of yard of your home.

Another: Write the petition, burn it in an ash tray. Add the ashes to an Adam & Eve or Come to Me Candle. Add a little bit of love powder to the candle. Add a little bit of love oil and dedicate to a desired entity or saint.

Protection Against Enemies

This is very simple. Write the persons' name on a piece of paper 4 times vertical, and 3 times on top horizontal. Then write or take a copy of a psalm that you like for overcoming enemies. Place the psalm on top of his/her name. Place his/her name on the ground in your back yard, the psalm on top of his/her name, and a big rock on top of both papers. Say: "As this rock and psalm lay heavy upon (his/her name), May he/she never be able to rise against me, hurt me, or jeopardize me and my job in any way. May anything wrong or bad that he/she tries to do against me fall upon he/her 10 times before it even touches me."

This work can be done for any reason that you would need to control or subdue an individual - Just change the petition or wording to fit the desire.

Simple Head Washing Ritual

Introduction:

This particular ceremony is used for removing curses, jinxes, or bad luck. It will bring blessings to the individual as a result of getting rid of the negative karma that they have been living.

This negative karma is an accumulation of negative vibrations absorbed in time, which has never been removed. Negative influences are accumulated in time due to stress, depression, anxiety, quarrels, fights, verbal/physical assault, justice situations, domestic violence, being cursed as well as cursing others. We also do harm to ourselves, as in pay for consequence of our actions. "He who is without sin, cast the first stone." The head washing is also followed by a head serving ritual.

Most Santeria priests-esses believe that these rituals should only be done by them, and that one should not be able to do it for oneself. True, if one wants to be as technical as a priest-ess. For this, one needs to be a priest and be trained as one. Yet, there are times and places where there is no Santeria priest readily available to perform the ritual. There are moments of desperation, solitude, sorrow, and of feeling disgraced. Where one wants to cry out for some kind of relief. What I say to this is, when there is no one around, there is oneself. It is better to do something to get a little bit of relief, than do nothing and get no relief. This is of course until one is able to reach or travel to someone that can conduct a proper head washing and head serving. This,

139

of course, if recommended via a divination reading as part of the prescribed healing therapy solution.

Head Washing Preparation

Ingredients:

Herbs: Sage, Mint, Spearmint, Peppermint, Ginger mint, Parsley, Rosemary, Watercress, Lettuce, Bay leaf, Basil, Oregano, Hibiscus, Jasmine, Fern, & Marjoram.

I recommend these herbs in lieu of the more traditional Lucumi herbs because there are places where the traditional Lucumi herbs are not readily available. So, one has to have the knowledge of what are more common herbs which can be sought out in almost any grocery, or plant nursery store, throughout the country.

Other Materials: Rum, Peace powder/efun/cascarilla, and Honey. White Soap cut into small cubes.

Procedure:

Boil plants in very large cooking pot. After boiling for about 15 minutes, let cool down. Once cooled, add half a cup of rum, 1 whole crushed cascarilla/peace powder, and finally honey. Remove the herbs by straining them out while pouring the bath water into a bucket. Add more water, if not enough to fill the bucket. The separated herbs are collected into a bowl. No stems, just crushed leaves.

Ritual Instructions:

Place a straw mat on the floor. At the top of the mat, place a large plastic bowl/tub. Something that will collect the bath water as it is being poured over your head. On a plate next to this tub, place a glass of water and candle. Place the bucket with the bath water next to the tub, easily accessible. Place a cup or small plastic bowl in the bucket of bath water. This is so that the water can be taken from the bucket, and poured over the head, when the time comes. Place the bowl with herbs and cubed soap, in front of the bucket with bath water easily accessible.

Stand in barefoot on the mat in front of the center tub or large bowl for collecting the bath water. To the right should be the bucket with bath water, and in front the bowl with cubed soap and herbs. Do a quick prayer as accustomed. Asking for God and the divine forces, spirit guides, and Orisha's to give you the grace for the effectiveness of this ritual. Now, kneel down take some herbs and soap with your left hand. Take the small bowl or cup and use to take from the bath water. Lower your head as far down as you can and proceed to washing your head with the soap and herbs while pouring the bath water on/over your head. Pray as you are accustomed to doing, asking that the energies of the herbs, soaps, and bath water to wash away, curse, envy, jealousy, witchcraft, curse, anger, depression, etc. You can do a "Lord's Prayer", "Hail Mary", "Glory Be to the Father", and any other prayers for expunging which you know.

Proceed for about 10-15 minutes, washing and rinsing your head with the bath water. When you stop put whatever

141

remaining soap & herbs you still have in your hand in the container full of soaped water. Continue rinsing your head a little bit with the bath water itself. Then, towel dry. The soaped dirty bath water can be tossed in the yard. You can also rinse with fresh clean water. Ritual is completed.

Other Books by blue ocean press

Selection of Prayers for Enlightenment

By Baba Sixto J. Novaton

Spirituality/Religion | ISBN: 978-4-902837-22-3

This work is intended for all those that wish to connect to spiritual divine energies, and forces. This is for those wishing to forge a relationship with ancestor, spirit guides, angels, divinities, and deities through devout spiritual devotion. It all begins with the erection of a spiritual altar, or shrine in your home. Dedicating one hour a week to solemn devoted prayer, this will soon become ritual, the ritual turns into a connection; and enlightenment is achieved. Once, enlightenment is achieved comes the next step, which is communication by way of divination. Through divination the communication, revelations, or messages become clarified, so verification and proof of your spirituality working is achieved. These selected prayers will nourish people's psyches, provide protection, and take people's spirituality to a higher level.

Baba Sixto was born in Cuba in 1961 and was brought to the United States in 1966, where he has lived all his life. He was initiated into the Cuban Yoruba Lucumi Santeria Religion as a Shango priest in 1977 in Miami. He worked as an Information Technology professional from 1979 to 2000. He was initiated as a Yoruba Lucumi Ifa priest in 1997 in Miami. He has been dedicated to full-time religious study and practice as an IFa priest since 2000. Baba Sixto has instructed many on how to build spirituality, connect to spiritual forces, so as to acquire the necessary intonation to then enter the Yoruba Lucumi Religion. Working as a Babalawo, Baba Sixto supports the well being of mankind through Yoruba Lucumi Ifa ritual healing therapies. He currently lives and works in Jacksonville, Florida. He also travels and attends to godchildren and clients in New York, Georgia, Texas, and Puerto Rico.

How To Order blue ocean press books

Books can be ordered directly from blue ocean press:

http://www.blueoceanpublications.com

Volume Discount:

<u>Individual Buyers</u>: If ordered from blueoceanpublications.com, an order of 5 or more of a single title receives a 30% wholesaler discount.

<u>Retail and Institutional Buyers</u>: Receive a 40% discount for purchases.

Please contact us at: **wholesale@blueoceanpublications.com** to receive the discounted invoice.

Blue ocean press titles can also be purchased at your neighborhood bookstore or ordered from the online bookstores, book distributors, and wholesalers listed below. They are also available at other fine brick & mortar and online retailers.

US:
Amazon.com, Barnes & Noble, Ingram, Baker & Taylor, NACSCORP, Espresso Book Machine

UK:
Adlibris.com, Amazon.co.uk, Bertrams, Blackwell, Book Depository, Coutts, Gardners, Mallory International, Paperback Shop, Eden Interactive Ltd., Aphrohead

Additional amazon.com sites:
Brazil: amazon.com.br; Canada: amazon.ca; China: amazon.cn; France: amazon.fr; India: amazon.in; Italy: amazon.it; Germany: amazon.de; Japan: amazon.co.jp; Mexico: amazon.com.mx; Spain: amazon.es

We also have printers in Australia, Germany, and Brazil, so titles can be ordered within the local book distribution system in Australia, Germany, and Brazil.